S0-ADE-404

VIC COBURN:

MAN WITH THE HEALING TOUCH

VIC COBURN:

Man With the Healing Touch

BY C. A. ROBERTS

THOMAS NELSON INC., PUBLISHERS
Nashville
New York

WITHDRAWN
by Unity Library

UNITY SCHOOL LIBRARY
UNITY VILLAGE, MISSOURI 64065

Copyright © 1975 by C. A. Roberts. All rights reserved under International and Pan-American conventions. Published by Thomas Nelson, Inc., Publishers. Manufactured in the United States of America.

Library of Congress Cataloging in Publication Data
Roberts, Cecil A.
    Vic Coburn: man with the healing touch.
    "Sermons by Vic Coburn": p.
    1. Coburn, Vic. 2. Faith-cure. 3. Sermons, American. I. Coburn, Vic.
BV3785.C554R6   269'.2'0924 [B]   75-12931
ISBN 0-8407-5090-0

DEDICATED TO C. A. III,

who may be my greatest fan;
and who loves to brag
about his father's books.

CONTENTS

CONTENTS

PREFACE

Years ago I read of a news reporter's response upon hearing John Jasper, the great negro minister, preach his famous sermon, "The Sun Moves." The reporter said, "At the end of the sermon I was standing and applauding along with the rest of the crowd. In applauding, I was not confirming that I believed the sun moved. My applause meant that I believed in John Jasper."

So that I will not be accused later of disguised subtleties, I want to state at the outset that I believe in Vic Coburn. I am convinced that Vic Coburn believes in what he is doing.

Although I do not hold that I deserve to write this book, I do believe that a book such as the one you are about to read deserves to be written. In courts of law a good lawyer will always bypass secondary issues and move to ultimate questions. Similarly, in the case of testing the validity and power of revealed Christianity what more ultimate (in the sense that it is ultimately crucial to all of us) question can be asked than this: "is God at work in the world today?" And what better source is there for discussion of this question than the faith healer, who not only says, "Yes" to the above question, but affirms that God's power can be touched, felt, seen and experienced by every human being?

Therefore, walk with me through these pages as we test the chain of revealed Christianity at either its strongest or weakest link—the contemporary faith healing emphasis as seen through the ministry of Vic Coburn, Los Angeles, California.

Before you finish this book, I hope you will concur that I have asked every question that should be asked of a minister such as Vic Coburn. And I think you will agree that he has been as open and direct as you could ever ask of one in his position.

I want to thank Sam Moore, publisher of *Thomas Nelson,* for supporting this book. Bill Cannon, editor in chief, was of inestimable value in his suggestions regarding the manuscript.

Neither of these men was asked to endorse all the theological presuppositions of the subject of this book. Their aim was simply to help make society more aware of a very significant facet of contemporary religious life in America.

My thanks must also be extended to Ann Pyle, my secretary, who worked tirelessly to help put this manuscript in proper form from first draft to final typing.

And, of course, my thanks to Vic Coburn in allowing me literally to pick both his brain and his heart through countless hours of taping sessions in order to make this manuscript possible.

I used the phrase "strongest or weakest link." Each reader will decide for herself or himself which of these she or he chooses.

Regardless of this choice, I am certain that every reader will conclude that Vic Coburn is, in fact, a man with a healing touch.

VIC COBURN:

MAN WITH THE HEALING TOUCH

CHAPTER I

"The Healing Touch"

I first met Vic Coburn at a rally in Wichita, Kansas, on March 17, 1974. It was a Sunday afternoon. I had difficulty finding the 2,200 seat auditorium which was located in a downtown Convention Center complex. This was to be Vic Coburn's first public appearance in the city. There had been little publicity for the crusade except for a thirty-minute television program featuring Vic the previous week.

I arrived thirty minutes early and found a standing room only crowd. Apart from an abundance of wheel chair cases and some people on crutches, it was an ordinary looking group—not the elite of the city, but certainly not the lower class that usually frequents healing services I have attended.

I was prepared for the worst. During my seminary days, I had written an extensive research paper on two of the more prominent faith healers of the fifties. One ultimately died of polio and the other died of acute alcoholism. Both, in my estimation had been kind hearted egomaniacs and religious hucksters of the lowest sort.

They both had always followed a similar pattern in their services. First, they would have about forty-five minutes of fast pitched jungle-like music complete with drums and tambourines. Next, the healer would lash forth with a harsh thrashing that all present were sinners and that all sickness and suffering was caused by sin.

Then, after a pause, during which the servant God announced that God was leading him to take the third offering of the evening, the service was brought to its climactic moment—the time for the healing line.

"God," thundered the healer, "had empowered him to heal all those who had repentance enough and faith enough."

Those who found themselves in the front of the healing line were fortunate. Most of them had been coming regularly to afternoon services to fill out healing cards. Each day they were told they must come every night until their name came up.

Each night names were not pulled at random from a hat, but were carefully screened to meet the required specifications. It was essential, if one was to be selected, that he have an illness that could not be readily detected by the naked eye. Instead, he must have an illness, like cancer of the stomach, that could be described to the audience in vivid terms. Of course, after prayer by the healer, the person would be able, without X-ray or the examination of a physician, to proclaim that the cancer had vanished right there on the spot!

Enter Vic Coburn. What happened in Wichita that Sunday afternoon did not wash away all my bad taste for faith healers in general, and the faith healing movement in particular. However, enough occurred that was unique that made me want to get to know Vic Coburn better.

First, there was no musical frenzy. Bob Daniels, who previously spent eight years with Oral Roberts and two years with Kathryn Kuhlman, led the group in two brief low-key songs.

Second, in less than ten minutes, Vic Coburn casually walked on the stage in bow tie and immaculate tuxedo. Without notes or podium, and in a soft spoken manner, he delivered a simple Biblical dissertation on what it meant to be a Christian. To this point not a word had been said about physical healing.

Next, the minister extended an invitation for people to come forward to be saved. Hundreds came forward. These were taken backstage to be counseled by the evangelist on what it meant to be converted.

While Reverend Coburn was gone an offering was taken; no big deal; just a regular passing of the plates. This was to be all that was said about money for the day. The evangelist had passed up a great "I'll pray if you pay" opportunity.

When Vic Coburn returned he still had a happy almost carefree attitude about him. He said a strange sounding thing! "Many of you are here without faith. That's O.K. Just shove your faith in neutral and I'll push you with mine."

After his next move, I saw the pitch coming. "Many of you are here today who need physical healing from God. I feel led to do something. I am simply going to sweep my hand across this entire crowd, and as my hand passes your way, you are going to experience the healing power of God."

I had never seen this before. It smacked of mass hypnosis. He did it. Then he said, "I want those of you who have just been healed to come up here and tell me what happened to you."

I was admittedly confused. On the one hand, it seemed like a cop-out. But on the other hand, there was an absence of the selectivity of the normal healing line.

This process took about a half hour. Finally we moved into the really spooky stage. What happened next left all my analysis up for grabs.

Vic took the microphone and began to pace silently back and forth across the stage. Soon he moved out into the congregation. He had an intent look on his face like he was searching all the faces for some special guest. All the while he was whispering, "Yes, Jesus, thank you, Master."

The following events either took the most careful planning of the Broadway stage or the lying lunacy of everyone present or the work of a master clairvoyant or some kind of perception that was, at least, beyond me.

He stopped and pointed to a young lady and told her to stand up. He then said, "I do not know you, but God has revealed to me that you do not and have never had hearing in one of your ears."

She confirmed that she could not hear out of her left ear. He pointed to her and said, "By the authority given me by Jesus Christ, I command hearing to come to that ear."

Then he walked to her and told her to put her finger in her good ear, which she did. He then began backing away from her saying, in a conversational tone, "If you can hear me say, 'praise the Lord.'"

He continued backing away until those about him could barely hear him. Still, at the right time, the girl would repeat, "Praise the Lord." At the fartherest distance, he switched his instruction to "Thank you, Jesus." The girl didn't miss a beat. The mother confirmed that the girl had not heard from that ear in eight years.

He then turned to another section and said, "There are several of you over here who have one leg shorter than the other. Come up on the stage."

Several responded. He seated the first person in a chair, and held out both legs. One was about three inches shorter than the other. He swung the microphone cord about his neck and held the legs out in both hands. He said, "I command this short leg to be healed." In seconds, both heels were together.

I was admittedly getting very uncomfortable. I found myself wishing I had a short leg so that I could go up and expose him.

The evangelist paused and looked out over the congregation. He asked, "I wonder if we have a skeptic present? If so, would you mind coming up here and assisting me?"

A man came up on the stage who identified himself as a chiropractor. Vic put another person in the chair who had one leg about four inches shorter than the other. He asked the chiropractor to examine the legs. It was obvious that the heels were about four inches apart.

Vic stood about twenty-five feet away and asked the chiropractor to hold the heels in his hands. He then said, "In the name of Christ, I command that leg to come out."

There was a silence across the crowd. People were standing to see. I was among them. The chiropractor said, "There they are!"

The crowd applauded. Vic smiled and walked across the stage. He told the young man in the chair to go home and praise the Lord for what had happened.

Soon the service was over. No healing line; no frenzy; no conditioning about sin or faith; no ifs or maybes;

in fact, no real prayers for the sick. Just a sermon, a few confident smiles, some strong commands and a touch.

It is a proven scientific fact that 80 percent of all sick people will ultimately get better with or without a physician. I remember spending a few weeks one time along the Amazon River in Brazil. The people in the area had never so much as seen an aspirin. Whenever someone was ill, they simply said he had the fever. Everyone always died of the same illness—"the fever." And yet, most of the people in the area, in time, usually recovered from "the fever."

Now it is also accepted that doctors and medicine can speed up the healing process and give order and structure to it.

But what about the healing touch?

CHAPTER II

"The Storm Before the Calm"

When the service was over in the Wichita Convention Center, I made my way across the street to a hotel which adjoined the Center. By prior arrangement I was to meet with Reverend Coburn about direct mail.

I rang his suite and was surprised to find him already there. He had slipped out during the closing prayer.

This is neither unusual nor unexpected. The man had been on stage for over two hours—two hours of what had to be enormous pressure; enough to cause emotional drain in the strongest. Futhermore, there are always some who feel they were slighted and who would keep a man as long as he would consent. There are other people who would not hesitate to tear a sleeve off the man's tuxedo in the name of God, and the interest of collecting significant religious relics.

The point I am making is that I knew the pilgrimage I was about to take up to the private quarters of Vic Coburn was one that would have been coveted by all of those people I had just left across the street. Here I was on my way into the private sanctuary of the fastest rising faith healer in America!

I should pause at this point and confess that it is a bit unfair to refer to a person like Vic Coburn as simply, or predominantly, a "faith healer." He sees himself as far more than this. And how he sees himself will surface in the later pages of this book.

But the truth of the matter is that Vic Coburn is predominantly a faith healer. That's how people who follow him see him. That's the area where his fame is rising, and this is the area where he has to field 95 percent of the questions about his ministry.

And the additional truth is that there is a tangible difference in the way people look upon ministers who are involved in overt efforts toward divine healing and those who are not.

I can vouch for this evaluation personally. If there is anyone who does *not* intimidate me or cause me to stand in awe, it is a minister. I spent fifteen years of my life in the active ministry. I preached to as large crowds as any other minister, and I knew more ministers—and more about ministers—than anyone else.

However, on my way up to Vic Coburn's suite on the top floor I had a new and unidentifiable lump in my throat. In previous years I had studied a great deal and also written a great deal about faith healers. Now I was on my way into the presence of a "live one."

I did everything possible to rationalize away the sense of uneasiness I felt as the elevator ascended, symbolically I surmised, above the city lights. It did not go away, and has not to this day even after I have established a fairly close personal relationship with Vic Coburn.

Maybe this isn't the time or place to discuss all this, but I feel that we are on the trail of something that the reader must "feel along with me" in order to get the most from this writing. So let me take a quick shot at what I mean and I'll move on.

There is an essential inherent difference in a "faith healing" minister and a "non-faith healing" minister. I don't know how else to say it. Certainly they are both purportedly God's men who are attempting to do God's work.

However, the "non-faith healer" can always hide his case in the unseen realm where God is mysteriously at work. The "faith healer", for better or worse, puts it all out on the line for all to see. He resents the very thought that there is anything God can't do. He doesn't take medicine or go to doctors.

I am rambling. Let me put it this way. Occasionally, Vic will ask me how I have been and I don't dare tell him! Once I was to meet him and couldn't go because I had a bad cold. My secretary, in canceling the appointment, had to think up a reason for me not to be able to come—that he couldn't pray for and correct right there on the phone!

I know I sound paranoid. Probably, Vic would have simply said in response to news about my cold, "I'm sorry. I hope he gets to feeling better."

I'm trying to tell you what was rushing through my mind as I reached the twenty-second floor of that hotel.

I knocked. Shortly, the door opened and I was face to face with Vic Coburn. The most predominant thing I recall about first seeing him up close was his eyes. I was tempted to say his smile but it is his eyes that set the face apart.

They dart, yet remain riveted. They probe, yet twinkle. I'll never forget his eyes.

Our first meeting lasted an hour. He was a gentleman in every way; polite, courteous; didn't hog the conversation. The "suite" was not as plush as one might expect. There was a small sitting room which was obviously used for work—a typewriter, several books, numerous papers, a Bible—and a small bedroom.

In that hour Vic Coburn exuded polish. He was ex-

tremely articulate, casually exhibiting a vocabulary
that smacked of Spiro Agnew. If all of this sounds a bit
overstated, it will appear even more incredible when
placed beside the younger Vic Coburn.

THE STORM

The birth took place in Yuma, Arizona. His parents
were never Christians nor even mildly religious
oriented. Young Vic, during all his early years, had
been exposed to no knowledge of, nor interest in, God.

By age fifteen, he had already been in and out of
reform school as well as several detention homes and
county jails. By this early age, he had already popped
pills; sniffed glue; been involved in several types of
crime; and had been suspended from school perma-
nently. Most of these activities had occured in Central
San Joaquin Valley around the town of Madera, California.

The area in which young Vic lived was called "Little
Oklahoma". It was filled with mean kids and Vic was
one of their leaders.

At age sixteen he ran away from home for over a
year. During this time he lived like a hippie, and this
was before the country had become familiar with the
term "hippie". As a result of this experience, Vic got
into so much trouble that the authorities gave him the
choice of either returning to live with his parents or
going to prison.

Vic made the necessary verbal commitments to return and realign himself with his probation officer.
Instead, he continued stealing automobiles and boozing
around with bad characters.

One day Vic went looking for an old friend of his in
"Little Oklahoma." He rode his motorcycle down to

the end of an irrigation canal where the boy had lived. When he found his friend, the boy told Vic that he had been saved. Vic responded by snickering sarcastically, since he didn't even know what the term "saved" meant. He asked his friend what he had been saved from.

The boy told Vic that he had accepted Jesus Christ as his personal Saviour at the old Southern Baptist church down the street from Merle's Store. He asked Vic to go to church with him.

At first Vic declined the invitation. Then he was told that a lot of pretty girls attended the church services and he changed his mind and consented to go.

This was one of the few times Vic had ever been inside a church. Once before he had attended a Catholic church and had caused so much commotion during the communion service that he was asked to leave.

He sat between his friend, Robbie, and a tall brunette Baptist girl in the church that day by Merle's Store. His only thought was that he was surrounded by a bunch of weird fanatics.

During the service something happened that Vic could not understand. He was experiencing his initial feelings of spiritual conviction. He was extremely uncomfortable and wanted to leave. He kept making loud and disturbing comments and the brunette kept telling him to "shut up."

When the service was over, the girl asked him if he would come back that night. Vic responded, "Are you kidding? Once a year is enough for me!"

The brunette said, "I'm going to be praying for you."

"Well, you just keep your prayers," Vic replied, filled with anger and disgust. He got on his bike and burned off for home.

Vic was supposed to go to a beer party that evening.

He thought all afternoon of the brunette's words. He decided he would ride by the church and "rap out the pipes of his bike" to let them know he was around.

He rode past the church. The door was open and he could see the people inside singing. He reversed the exhaust on his bike as he passed, creating a loud roar. He grinned from ear to ear and rode on down to Merle's Store. Across the street was Melvin's Garage. He turned around at the gas pumps and started back past the church to give them one more blast for good measure.

Pausing at the gas pumps, he began thinking of a night two weeks earlier. He had been staying downtown in an old $2.00 motel room on the second floor.

At three o'clock in the morning, he lay in the bed unable to sleep. The red and orange neon lights across the street kept flickering through the broken venetian blinds. He lay there lonely, tired, and frustrated. He had no money, no job, no education, no future, no hope—nothing.

In the dark he lay with tears coming down his cheeks. Inside he was crying out, "I wish there was a God to believe in; I wish there was somebody bigger than me to trust in." Finally, he fell asleep, convinced there was no one and nothing to believe in.

Before realizing it, Vic was back in front of the church. He pulled into the driveway, parked his bike and walked in the front door of the church. There sat the brunette. She had saved a place for him. Unknown to Vic, they had been praying all afternoon that he would be saved that night.

Vic once again began trying to disturb the service, but the girl gently restrained him. The preacher began his sermon. He was an old hell-fire and damnation minister.

Vic began to detect a conspiracy. It sounded to him like someone had told the preacher everything he had ever done wrong.

The sermon was over and everyone stood for the invitation. They began singing, "All Ye Who Are Weary, Come Home." Although Vic was only a teenager, he sat there feeling weary and old inside. For the first time in his life, he wanted God. His head was bowed. He was gritting his teeth to keep from crying. Inwardly he said, "God, if all this isn't just a lot of religious pretense and nonsense, then let me feel something."

At that very moment, a hand gripped his shoulder. Cold chills ran up his spine. At first, he thought it was God's hand. He looked up and there stood the old preacher, tears streaming down his face, asking Vic if he would come to Christ.

Vic stepped into the aisle, almost ran to the altar, and fell on his knees. He didn't know how to pray. A few weeks earlier, to his friends, he had cursed the name of God. He had dared God to strike him dead. He had bragged openly about his atheism. Now he was on his knees asking the God he had cursed to save him and change his life.

There was no flash of light; no burst of thunder. But deep in his heart there came a confidence that his sins were forgiven and that Christ had come into his heart.

When Vic stood to his feet, tears streaming down his face, he saw a line of people waiting to speak to him. They knew who he was and had been praying for him for a long time.

A woman about seventy-five years old came by, took Vic's hand in hers, and said, "Son, you don't know who I am, but I know who you are. I've been praying for you for three months. Every time I heard you going by my house, I would get down on my knees and pray that God would save your soul."

The woman continued in a way that caught Vic unprepared. "Son, God is going to make a preacher out of you."

Vic wanted to say, "You're wrong, lady; God couldn't make a preacher out of me," but it was too late. She was gone, with those last words still hanging in the air ". . . a preacher out of you."

THE STORM CONTINUES

During the next several months, Vic did everything possible to live for Christ. His life was such a flaming testimony of God's love and power that his parents, friends, and even his probation officer had trouble believing that this was the same Vic.

A year passed and Vic entered the army. Although he began his military days trying to win everyone to Christ, within a period of months the tide began turning. Vic began, like Jonah, running from God. He knew in his heart that God was calling him to preach. But how could this be true? He had no formal education. He knew that preachers had college and seminary degrees.

In his heart, he knew he was rationalizing: that his efforts at preaching to that point had been well received. There had been a particular Sunday, shortly after his conversion, a Youth Sunday. Vic had preached the night service. He had prayed all afternoon.

That night, he stood and preached for about ten minutes from the Book of Matthew—about the mote and beam in a person's eye. Suddenly, in the midst of his sermon Vic began to cry. He continued trying to preach, but kept breaking up, weeping uncontrollably.

He finally stopped preaching and extended the invitation for people to come to Christ. An entire family of seven stepped forward, followed by others, all accepting Christ. It was the most conversions the church had seen on a Sunday night in its history.

Now, he was in the army and began to experience the power of Satan to lead a young Christian to backslide.

In very little time, Vic went AWOL from the army and was sent to the prison in Fort Carson, Colorado. It was there that Vic tried to turn his back on both his conversion and his calling. He incited a riot at Fort Carson and was put in maximum security. His new home was called a "Rabbit Cage." It was about six feet wide and ten feet long. For two weeks he was fed nothing but lettuce and bread.

The military decided that Vic was a hopeless case. The decision was made that he would be given a dishonorable discharge and be immediately sent to Fort Leavenworth, Kansas, for two years in prison.

Sometimes a person can see the providence of God in action only as he looks back. That morning in Fort Carson, God's hand was obviously at work.

Vic was up early, as he had been instructed. As soon as his papers were completed, he would be on his way to Fort Leavenworth and two years of prison.

There was a knock on his door. Three armed guards stood before him. "This is it," Vic thought.

"We have orders to return you to your base in California."

The three men took Vic to the stockade commander, and told him they had orders to return Vic to California. By a strange coincidence, these three guards were friends of Vic's from previous days.

"But we are making final preparations to send Coburn to Fort Leavenworth."

"Are the papers completed for that particular transfer?" one of the three guards inquired. He was given a negative reply.

"Then, since our papers are complete, I suggest that the prisoner be placed in our custody."

The stockade commander complied, and Vic was on his way back to California with his three friends. He had escaped prison.

But the storm was by no means over for Vic, for he was still a fugitive from God's will and there is no peace for such a person ". . . Wither shall I flee from Thy Presence, and wither shall I run from Thy Mercy; if I ascend into the highest heavens, Thou art there; if I make my bed in hell, Thou art there; if I take the wings of the morning and fly to the ends of the earth, behold, Thou art there."

Vic was assigned to another company, but his problems remained the same as before. He was a young man on the run from God!

He wouldn't go to work; he wouldn't make his bed; he had quit from the inside out.

One night Vic found himself in a beer parlor. He was hopelessly floundering. He cared for nothing. In his pocket, he had a full bottle of high potency nerve pills. He slumped into a booth and began ordering beer. Two of the pills in his bottle were strong enough to put a person out. And, of course, it was almost suicide for a person to consume alcoholic beverage at the same time he was consuming narcotics.

Vic sat at the table, drinking a beer, and then taking a couple of pills; then more beer; then more pills. In a few hours the pills were gone, as were a dozen bottles of beer. Vic fell from the booth to the floor. No one in the parlor moved. To them, Vic Coburn was just another slobbering drunk. With his mind fading in and out like a faulty radio reception, Vic began to crawl toward the door. When he could finally feel the cool cement of the outside pavement, he passed out.

A half-hour later, some of the guys from Vic's company came by, saw him lying on the sidewalk, and carried him back to his company. He was still out. One of the sergeants found the empty pill bottle in his pocket and thought he had attempted suicide. Someone called an ambulance and carried him to the hospital.

Vic regained consciousness three days later. His stomach had been pumped out just in time. The doctor said his system had enough barbituates in it to kill a mule, even without the alcohol.

The nerve pills had done their damage, creating a total nervous breakdown. His entire body went haywire on the fourth day. An Assembly of God chaplain came by to see him. He talked straight to the young renegade.

"Son, you have a call of God on your life, don't you?" he asked. Vic lay staring at him, saying nothing, but wondering who had been talking to him. The chaplain continued.

"Look, you're going to die if you don't surrender your heart and life to God's call. I'm going to pray that God will let you get out of this hospital alive, but only if you will promise me that you will come to my Thursday night Full Gospel Servicemen's Service at the chapel."

Vic said he would, not meaning it. In a few days he was out of the hospital and feeling fine. He was reassigned to his company and Thursday night he was back at the beer parlor. The Fourth Brigade Chapel was down the street and he decided to stop by.

He came into the service late and sat down behind a

tall M.P. Vic had always hated cops in any form. But this one kept saying, "Praise God! Hallelujah!"

There was a group from one of the local churches singing. He began to have the same sensations he had the night at the church down by Merle's Store. He knew this was the night he was going to have to surrender his life totally to God.

Without waiting for the invitation, Vic ran to the front and fell on his knees, weeping and praying. The chaplain came and put his arms around him. For two hours he stayed on his knees. He thought his insides were going to burst.

He begged God to forgive him. When the service was over, Vic walked to the back of the chapel. A tract caught his eye. It was a Billy Graham tract entitled, "Peace With God." He took it from the rack and read it carefully. "That's the message I want to preach to others," he said to himself.

THE CALM

From that night, a genuine peace began to settle upon Vic's life. There would be many more hills to climb and battles to fight, but this time he was truly on his way in his spiritual journey. Vic Coburn had finally been wounded of the Lord; a wound from which he would never recover. His experience, this time, was for real, although it was still destined to become more intense.

By another stroke of good fortune, Vic's undesirable discharge was put aside. Instead, he was given an honorable medical discharge—the medical resulting from his bout with the beer and pills.

Within several weeks, Vic was home again, this time as a very active young minister. He was given the opportunity to be a Youth for Christ director, working with one of the Southern Baptist churches in the area.

From the very beginning, Vic's preaching was met with unusual results. Large numbers would come forward in every service making public decisions to accept Christ. Young people, many drawn by Vic's "pre-conversion fame," came to hear the young evangelist. There was little doubt from the outset of his preaching that here was a young man with unique and abundant drawing power as a soul winner.

But what was happening went deeper than this. Vic had a job at this time selling carpet and draperies. He worked with a boy who was a member of a Full Gospel church in town. This was a Pentecostal church. Vic was very suspicious of Pentecostals, what he knew of them, which wasn't a lot. He thought they were all migrants from Arkansas, Oklahoma, and Texas, drove old beat up used cars and picked cotton for a living.

Vic began attending the Penecostal church with his friend from work. It was at this point that the young minister began searching out the meaning of being filled with the Spirit. For weeks he studied the Bible and prayed for God's power to fall on his life in the greatest possible way.

When it happened, he did not know what to call it: Baptism of the Holy Spirit; Being Filled with the Spirit; Immersion of the Spirit. Vic knew something new and different had happened. His life was dramatically changed in ways that were difficult to explain.

STORM WITHOUT CALM WITHIN

His pastor at the Baptist church was very upset with Vic, as were some of his minister friends. These men who had prayed so hard for his conversion were afraid he was carrying things too far. They told him he couldn't help anybody by becoming a religious fanatic. Vic had no reason not to believe them so he tried to tone down his feelings. It didn't work. He felt there was a new power in his life that could not be denied.

Vic decided to stand by his experience and was kicked out of the church where he had been serving. A couple of weeks later, he was invited to preach a youth crusade at one of the large Full Gospel churches in the area.

Vic was bursting to preach. The first two nights saw many people saved. There was great emotion in the services, but things were not yet completely in focus.

On the third night, an event occurred which turned out to be possibly the most significant experience in Vic's entire ministry. He turned a final corner that night. From this point forward, there would be no return.

Vic was sitting on the platform during the singing when he heard a Voice say, "There is a man in the back of the auditorium and he has a back brace on. If you will call him forward, I will heal him."

Vic turned, thinking someone in the choir had spoken to him. No one responded the way they should if they had been "The Voice."

"The Holy Spirit just spoke to me," Vic thought to himself. He waited for the Holy Spirit to say something else. He didn't say anything else.

Vic leaned over to the pastor and said, "The Holy Spirit just spoke to me."

The minister looked at him and said, "Well, yeah."

Vic said, "Pastor, God really did speak to me. I must obey Him."

He said, "Alright. Do what you have to do."

"I stepped up to the pulpit and said, 'Folks, I'm fresh

out of a Southern Baptist church. I've been very conservative. I'm not a fanatic and I'm not crazy.

'But I just heard the Voice of God . . . Don't ask me to explain it. I don't even know how to talk about the gifts of the Spirit. All I know is that I heard the Voice of God telling me something'. . .

"I saw a man in the back in about the second from the last pew with a plaid shirt on . . .

"That's the man!" Vic pointed to a man in the back and said, "Sir, don't ask me how I know this, but you have a back brace that I can't see through your clothing. You have a serious problem and if you will come forward, God's going to heal you."

The man shot out of his seat and ran to the front. He took his back brace off. He could touch his toes. He could do calisthenics. The man told the people he had been on disability for three years. There was no question in the man's mind. He had been healed.

CHAPTER III

"Vic, The Pastor"

The night of Vic's first major healing, people came up to him after the service saying, "Son, you know you have a great gift from God."

The pastor of the church was skeptical. So were the other preachers who talked to Vic. They told him not to get too emotionally involved with the idea of healing. Some told him about healers who had gone bad. Others told him he would soon be preaching false doctrine. There was not one preacher who appeared to be excited or glad over what was happening to Vic.

Since no one else had any faith in him, Vic decided to have faith in himself. He prayed daily for a faith to heal. He prayed nightly for people and they were healed. His gift was not as consistent or creative at this stage as it would be later, but amazing things were happening.

The same pattern developed every week. Vic would see tremendous things happen at night when he preached. However, the people close to him didn't accept it. They were skeptical and critical.

It was a lonely experience for·the young minister. For a full year nothing changed. Vic continued to go from church to church holding revivals. People continued to be healed, and the pastors of the churches continued to be critical, cautious, and skeptical of this young minister with his peculiar gifts.

At the end of this difficult year, Vic married, and shortly after that, became pastor of a small church. He was twenty years old. The church was not large enough to support a pastor full time. They paid him $10.00 a week. There were twenty members in the church. Vic had an extra job driving a diesel truck.

Since his heart was more in his church work than driving a diesel, Vic decided to stop driving and pastor the church full time.

When he announced his decision to the deacon board, they almost had a collective heart attack. They said they couldn't afford to pay him what he would need to live. Vic told them he would settle for a tithe of the offering.

He quit his job and told his wife he was going to start fasting and praying until he heard from God. He had been seeing healings, but he wasn't satisfied. He had found himself going about his ministry with too much caution, too little faith. He would pray for people and then "hope" that something would happen.

He knew that the ministry of Jesus and his disciples had been one of power and authority. They spoke healings. They commanded miracles to happen. There was no "ifs" or "maybes"; no pleading and hoping. "In the name of Christ I command you," the disciples would say, "to be healed!"

Vic attended some of the meetings of men who claimed to have the healing power of God, expecting to witness the power and authority he read about in the scripture. He did not see what he had hoped to see. Instead, he heard men talk about what had happened the night before; and what was going to happen the next night. But nothing ever happened right that moment.

The young minister made a decision that set the

Sight is restored to the blind left eye of a man.

Crowds attend a Vic Coburn Crusade.

The short leg of
this man is healed.

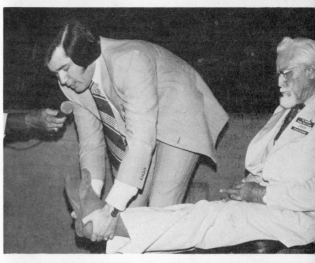

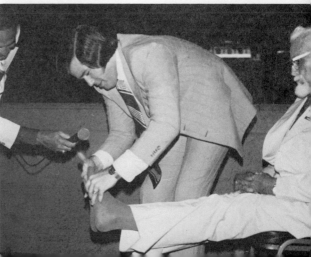

pace for his ministry. He determined that he was going to have a Jesus ministry of authentic spiritual power. If he couldn't have this, he was going to forget the whole thing. He didn't want a sham ministry. He knew God had given him an ability to win souls. He could be successful as a soul winner.

He did not have to be a healer. He did not desire this sort of thing to be a "big shot" in people's eyes. He only wanted to make an impression for Jesus. He wanted to convince people of the resurrected reality of Jesus Christ. Certainly he could win people to Christ! Why could he not also set people free from sickness and suffering, and the powers of Satan?

Vic told his wife he was going to pray all night long every Monday night. He would go to the church at six o'clock in the evening and would pray until 6:00 A.M. Tuesday. All night long he would lay across the altar at the front of the church. The rest of the mornings during the week Vic would set his alarm at five o'clock in the morning. His parsonage was in the basement of the church. He would arrive before sunrise and pray until 9:00 A.M. After this, Vic would have a light breakfast and then go out visiting people who needed Christ.

Vic would always spend his afternoons in prayer. Soon, deciding this wasn't enough, he also began spending his afternoons in prayer at the church.

Soon he quit eating. This is commonly known in spiritual circles as fasting. Starvation plays strange tricks on the body. Vic began losing weight. He grew weak and sick. One morning, his weakness finally overcame him. He could not raise himself from bed. He crawled on his hands and knees to the kitchen to get a drink of water. His wife was crawling right behind Vic, begging him to eat something. She was genuinely afraid he was going to die.

Vic was praying for two things: he wanted God to fill his church and he wanted a miracle ministry. He had been having about fifteen to twenty people at church on Wednesday evenings.

It was on a Wednesday evening that Vic lay face down on the floor, trying to catch his breath, unable to continue his painful journey for water. As he lay there, an experience he had earlier that day was flooding his mind.

He had been walking in the church auditorium while he prayed over and over the same prayer, "God give me this power. I don't know what it's going to cost. But Lord, I'm willing to give you anything I have for the anointing that I believe is necessary to reach this nation for Your glory."

He was standing about ten feet from a wall furnace when it happened. To Vic it was the Voice of God as surely as he was alive. "My Son," the Voice said to Vic, "freely you have received. Now, freely give."

The words were to Vic the revelation he had been waiting for. God was saying that everything he was praying for had already been given, and it was free. He couldn't buy it. But it was already there to be claimed and used.

Immediately he had fallen to his knees and prayed, "God, if You really mean that I have what I've been praying for, then tonight in the service do something that You have never done before—give me people! Bring people from everywhere! I want the biggest crowd that I've ever had on Wednesday night to confirm this to me."

Now, as he lay on the floor in his apartment below

the church, the experience seemed dim to his memory. Soon he faded into unconsciousness, totally exhausted.

About 7:00 P.M., he was awakened by a strange new and unusual sound. He heard footsteps above him on the hardwood floor of the church above him. He raised himself to his knees and listened closer. There was no single sound, but many sounds, clicking of heels, muffled voices. "Could it be?" he asked himself.

A deacon ran down the steps and into the room where his preacher was now standing. "Brother Vic, you've gotta come up there and see. There are people everywhere! People from all over the country are in the service tonight!"

Vic quickly dressed, forgetting temporarily how weak he was. In no time, he was in the pulpit looking out over his packed house. He was thrilled. This was God's confirmation. He was soon into his sermon, preaching with great vitality. This was not to last. In a few minutes, the long hours and days of fasting took their toll.

Beads of sweat popped out on Vic's forehead. He tried to ignore what was happening. It was too late. He passed out, taking the pulpit with him to the floor. The people crowded around him thinking he had had a heart attack. In a few seconds he began regaining consciousness. He was flat of his back looking up at a circle of faces.

He struggled to his feet, picked up the pulpit and stood leaning against it. He tried to speak. Instead, tears filled his eyes and he was weeping uncontrollably. All he could say was, "Why don't you come and pray." Soon, every person in the church was on his knees praying.

Much later that night, Vic stood alone in the darkness of the church. He now knew for certain what had been there all the time. He knew why he had rebelled after his conversion. He knew why he had been so restless. Now it was clear. He now knew that God had a call in his life; something greater that he had ever realized. At this point, he did not know how to explain it. He was experiencing something like trying to yawn, or take a deep breath, and not completely be able to fulfill the exercise.

Vic knew God was leading him, but where? He knew God was releasing unto him power, but in what form? and for what purpose? when? where? how?

It seemed that for every answer Vic received from God at this early stage there would follow a dozen more questions. He knew he was on the right track. But standing there in the darkness, he was frustrated because he could not look into the future and see the shape his ministry would take.

One thing Vic could see that night, even in the dark —the past—his days of running; his days before God. And of this one thing he was certain: there would be no turning back!

CHAPTER IV

"The Gift of Faith"

Have you found yourself saying at this point in Vic's story, "Well, he's finally got it all together." If this is your response, then prepare yourself for some more ups and downs.

Perhaps it will help you in your understanding of Vic Coburn if you will realize that there were some things happening *inside* Vic Coburn and other things happening *around* him.

On the *outside,* God was preparing Vic for a ministry as an evangelist. The road Vic took toward a national evangelistic ministry was a rocky one. He had to encounter many hardships, setbacks, and failures. This process was not inconsistent with the way God has always developed His servants. There is not a prophet in the Old Testament who knew only success in an outward way. Some had to hide in caves; others were put in dens and prisons; one was dropped into a well.

What was happening to Vic on the *inside* was something else. It was here on the inside that God was developing the "Healing Touch." This is the part of Vic's experience that has only grown deeper for Vic, more astonishing to his followers, and more difficult to explain for his critics.

Before we proceed with the external accounting of the way God opened the doors to evangelism, let's take a closer look at what Vic calls "THE GIFT OF FAITH." Let Vic speak for himself:

THE GIFT OF FAITH

"During the early part of my evangelistic ministry, I went to a large church to conduct a crusade. I had driven all night to get there for the opening Sunday morning service. The church had been advertising for weeks that a young man of faith and power was coming to conduct a great healing meeting. The church was packed that morning and everyone was greatly excited about the crusade.

"I was so tired from traveling all night that I decided just to preach and dismiss the service without praying for the sick, but about the time I decided to dismiss the service—I noticed a hopeless looking man in a wheelchair in the back of the church that someone had just rolled in.

"I thought to myself, 'I'm sure glad that I don't have to pray for that man this morning,' but all of a sudden the pastor stepped up and told the audience that they had just brought this man from the hospital for Brother Coburn to pray for him. I almost passed out! I thought, 'OH NO!' 'Not upon the first service of the crusade, and especially not the way I feel now.'

"I felt completely faithless! I was almost scared to death. The pastor went on to tell the audience about what a great man of faith and power I was—and how he knew that I could pray the prayer of faith to help this helpless man. The ushers rolled the man to the front of the church. I had never seen such a pathetic case before in one of my meetings. His entire body was eaten up with cancer and he couldn't walk. As I stepped off the platform—my knees felt weak and perspiration popped out in the palms of my hands. My heart was crying out for faith and spiritual power. I knew that I didn't have enough faith for this man's deliverance. My heart was filled with fear instead of faith! When I reached the man, I circled his wheelchair a few times trying to find enough faith and courage to pray for him. But, there was no use I didn't have any faith, especially not enough faith to raise this man out of a wheelchair. Once again, I cried out to God in my heart. I said, 'God, if I ever needed a confirmation of your calling in my life—I need it now! I don't have enough faith, God.' All of a sudden (and I really can't explain this) but it felt just like someone pulled a plug in my soul, and drained out every fear, and all my doubts. Then He poured into my heart the overflowing power of "THE GIFT OF FAITH."

"I looked at this hopeless dying man, no longer as an impossible case—but I saw through the eyes of faith —a man who in just a few moments would be healed by the mighty power of God. I looked at the pastor and told him to hold onto the wheelchair because I was going to pray and pull the man out. And then I turned to the man himself, and said, 'Mister, I am going to speak a miracle to your body in the name of Jesus Christ, and you are going to walk. And, if you don't walk—I will drag your kneecaps off!!'

"When I layed hands on him I felt absolutely NOTHING! But the faith of God doesn't have to feel anything—real faith demands it done, with or without feeling! After laying hands on him I reached around his wrist, and around his arms, and pulled him completely out of the wheelchair. I expected him to walk immediately, but he didn't! Instead, he just hung limp over my arms. The devil seemed to whisper, 'you have really made a fool of yourself now. You had better set him back down while you can.'

"But I knew he was healed. Therefore, I whispered back, 'devil, you are a liar!! I know God has healed him!'

"So, I kept on dragging him away from his wheelchair, until I was almost running with him. The pastor looked like he was about to lose his false teeth, but I kept on dragging him across the church.

"All of a sudden I began to notice that he was becoming lighter and lighter and lighter. I looked down and he was running along beside me. HE WAS HEALED!!! I took his hand and we ran around the church several times. In a few days this man was driving his automobile and didn't look like the same man! But whose faith was it that healed this man? It wasn't mine, because I have already confessed that I was completely faithless, it was the faith of God!!!"

"In the 11th chapter of Mark, we read where Jesus and His disciples were on their way to Jerusalem. He was hungry and seeing a fig tree afar off, and expecting fruit to be on the tree, Jesus came to the tree, but it was fruitless. He then spoke to the tree and said, 'From this day, no man shall eat of your fruit.' I am sure the disciples wondered why Jesus cursed the fig tree, but they continued their journey to Jerusalem. The next day they passed by the same fig tree and it was withered from its roots up. It had died completely. Peter exclaimed to the other disciples' 'look, how soon the tree has withered!' Then Jesus turned to His disciples and said these marvelous words, 'Have the faith of God!' Jesus literally said to His disciples, men with God's faith, these things are possible. 'For verily I say unto you, whosoever shall say unto this mountain, be thou

This man has been healed.
He and his wife rejoice.

A healed woman carries
away her crutches at the
Prayer.

A healed man walks again after having been confined to a wheel chair.

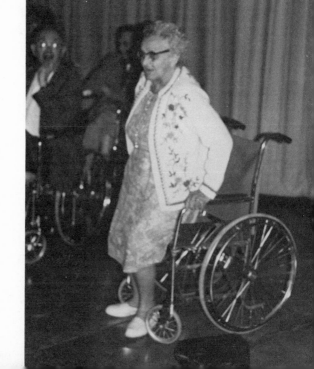

A woman forsakes her wheel chair after years of use.

removed, and be thou cast into the sea; and shall not doubt in his heart, but shall believe that those things which he saith shall come to pass, he shall have whatsoever he saith!'

"Did Jesus really mean that a person anointed by God could remove mountains? YES, A THOUSAND TIMES YES! Some would have us believe that Jesus meant spiritual mountains, problems in our lives. He did mean that, but He also meant that with the faith of God, that person could literally move mountains! Jesus would never have offered the faith of God to you and me as His followers, if He did not intend for us to have this faith and use it.

"My entire ministry depends upon the power of the faith of God. I have seen many other people receive and experience this same thing.

"I remember one night, a Methodist woman came to me for prayer. She had many things wrong with her body. When I asked her if she believed that God was going to heal her, she said, 'No, I don't!' I said, 'You don't?' She said, 'NO.' I told her to go back and sit in the audience and wait a few more nights until the Word of God and healings she witnessed built faith for her healing. That night I preached on the faith of God, and something happened because the very next night, she came before me for prayer.

"I hardly recognized her. She looked completely different. There was a glow of the Spirit of God on her face. She walked up to me and said, 'Reverend, I am ready now to be healed!' I said 'You are? I thought you didn't have any faith.' She said, 'I didn't before, but I do now. All I want you to do is lay hands on me, whether you believe or not, I believe, and I know I am going to be healed.' I had to laugh and rejoice at the same time.

"Where did this woman get such faith? The night before she was totally faithless, but this night she came believing with great, bold, daring faith. It was the faith of God. It was the anointing of 'THE GIFT OF FAITH!' "

THE MAKING OF AN EVANGELIST

The experiences related above became fairly regular in their occurance, even during the early stages and months of Vic's ministry. Consequently, he did not question the fact that God's power was operating in his life.

However, Vic had another matter that troubled him deeply. Unsaved people simply did not come to churches. On any given night, he could have a house full of Christians. However, he wanted to preach the gospel to the unsaved. And these people simply did not attend services in churches.

Vic would drive through a town and see a fairground building or a civic auditorium and something inside him would almost burst: "That's where I could get people out to hear the gospel," he would say to himself.

He would find himself sitting around thinking: "The unsaved don't come to church. And if they did, the churches aren't big enough to hold them. I must go out to a neutral ground where the unsaved will not mind coming."

Vic decided to become a crusader. He decided to hold his first "City-Wide" crusade in a little town called Chowchilla, California. There were several problems. First, he had no knowledge of how to plan a crusade. Second, he had no staff to help him. He decided to do it all himself. He rented the fairgrounds auditorium, printed a couple of thousand handbills, and contacted a few churches and asked for their support.

The crusade was a total loss. The largest crowd only half-filled the auditorium. The offerings were pitiful. Vic didn't get nearly enough money to cover his expenses.

Don't forget to keep the external and internal separate in your thinking. Even during this crusade with budget problems and small crowds, people who came continued to respond and the power of God was apparently at work.

Probably at this stage of Vic's ministry, God was having to work double time on the young evangelist's patience. Vic was in a hurry. He wanted to see the world won yesterday. And when things did not live up to his expectations, he had a tendency to think God had let him down.

That's exactly how he felt the Sunday afternoon he finally closed down the crusade in Chowchilla. At this time, Vic had a new pick-up and a twenty-four foot trailer home. So he climbed in his pick-up and left town. He drove without stopping for about three hours. The sun was going down. He turned off the main highway onto a dirt road so that he could look at the sunset. He slowed his truck to about five miles an hour.

"I just looked at that sunset and thought to myself, 'if God can make a sunset like that, why can't God help me do the work that I feel called in my soul to do? I don't have an education; I don't know how to plan crusades; but I know this is what God called me to do!'

"I stopped the pick-up and sat staring at that sunset and I heard the Voice of God. I do not know if it was an angel of God; I don't know if it was Jesus; but there was a Voice right there beside me—and it was an audible Voice—and this Voice said, 'I'm with thee!' That's all. 'I'm with thee.'

"And I just began to weep. I felt like a dam had

burst in my soul. I drove back to town with a new determination never to know doubt. Never—not one time—never, since that sunset, have I ever doubted that God was with me."

EUREKA!

It was about six months later that Vic conducted what could be called his first really successful crusade in Eureka, California. There were big crowds, many saved and healed, and good offerings, enough to meet the budget.

It was at this point he had to learn something about holding crusades; namely, that they would probably never pay for themselves if they were handled properly. That may sound strange, but it is the plain truth. An evangelist can always meet the budget if he stays inside the churches, because his crowd is mainly Christian, people who are in the habit of giving.

However, when an evangelist moves to neutral territory—such as a city auditorium, he can expect an increase in the percentage of unsaved present, but a decrease in giving per person.

This has always been true of the very best and most successful evangelists. Billy Graham always spends in the neighborhood of $250,000 for every crusade and always loses money (so says George Wilson, Executive Director of The Graham Organization).

This makes perfect sense. If an auditorium seats 10,000, it is a proven fact that you must invest so much per seat in preparation, rent, and advertisement, if you hope to fill the place consistently. And it will be victory enough if the place is filled. But an evangelist must anticipate that for every unsaved person (or empty seat) he must find additional financing.

So in these early days, Vic was just getting his taste

of the struggle to finance the gospel. It was, is, and always shall be a thankless task for any evangelist. People are so quick to criticise those who ask for money, yet are also very slow to say, "Thanks for trying to reach the world for Christ."

And let me pause a moment to add a personal note. I work with over twenty evangelistic organizations across the nation. I know enough about the inner workings of a dozen well-known evangelists to see whatever shortcomings there might be. I must say that I do not personally know of one of these men who takes advantage, for personal gain, of the money given to his ministry. I am not saying such persons don't exist. I just don't have personal knowledge.

What I am saying is that in my book, evangelists as a whole are a pretty special breed. If I didn't believe in the things they preach, I would still have to admire the ones I have come to know personally.

They have none of the advantages of a pastor. They have no built-in crowd; they have no group that pledges their annual budget in advance; they have no guarantee regarding their own salary.

As I see it, after spending over twenty years related to religious work, every minister has to make one of two choices: either a ministry geared toward security, but controlled by others; or a ministry of freedom, which carries with it numerous insecurities. This being the case, the "security-control" ministers usually end up as pastors, while the "freedom-insecurity" group usually gravitates toward evangelism.

In case you are missing my point, I am saying most pastors of churches have chosen security at all cost, while most evangelists have had the nerve . . . or faith . . . or guts to choose a free and unencumbered ministry, even though it might mean living from one day to the next in total uncertainty regarding tangibles.

I am not building a case against pastors; there just aren't very many I have known—and I've known a lot, having been at one time president of 35,000 of them—that I admire. And those few I do admire are exceptions to the above. The rule still stands for me.

BACK TO VIC

"I say all this to say," is a terrible phrase to use, so I'll discard it. I admire evangelists, even some that I don't like. It does not bother me to know Vic began a struggle early for money to finance his ministry. I'm only glad that God didn't tell him about T.V. in those early years. He wouldn't know what a hungry money-eating monster really looked like until he began, years later, the task of paying for T.V. productions and time. Here's how Vic speaks of those early months of getting started in crusades.

"I had to let some of my own personal bills get behind to pay bills for my crusades, and for my coordinator's expenses. Even my wife had serious doubts that God had really called me to this type ministry.

"My friends doubted too. They told me I was just on an ego trip, trying to build a name for myself. For five months I fought devils, my wife, my friends, everybody. They all said the same thing: 'what if the funds don't come in?'

"I said, 'if I have to go beg for it, I know one thing: God called me to this ministry. And somewhere out there are those who will help me. God's going to show me how to organize better and how to get cooperation.'

" 'In time,' Vic continued, 'the meetings began to grow.' Many thousands began to be saved, thousands baptised by the Holy Spirit. I've seen as many as ten blind people in one service get their sight back. I've seen eight or ten wheelchair cases in one service rise and walk by the power of God.' "

"But, I've never reached the place where I feel totally content and satisfied in my own spiritual life. And if there is one fear that I have, it is that I would fall short of what God expected of me.

"After years of work, I've been able to improve on the Vic Coburn of those early years. I've been able to accumulate greater knowledge; I've worked to build a better vocabulary. Sometimes, people even think I am a fairly educated man.

"I say all this because I don't think God hands any-one anything free. It has been a long, hard uphill battle to make this ministry the ministry I feel God ordained it to be. But I believe God gives a man an option when He calls him. I know some men who have great ability and potential for success, but they would not pay the price for success.

"I believe God expects His servants to pray as though it all depends on God, and work as though it all depends on them. That's why I work as hard as I do. I'm not afraid I will disappoint men; only God."

CHAPTER V

"What Makes a Faith Healer Tick?"

You must forgive me for the choice of title for this chapter, but it was selected only after much agonizing over a question that has haunted me for twenty years; namely, "what makes a faith healer tick?"

The year selection of twenty years actually dates back to the year 1957, a year when I did an extensive study of the faith healing movement, which was much alive in America at that time, primarily being carried on by Oral Roberts, A. A. Allen, and Jack Coe. Before this book is completed, much of my search of twenty-years past will find its way into these pages.

Perhaps I should tackle the question as to what made me tick when I first did the study on healing. There were several factors: first, I wanted to know, if possible, just what were the limits or margins of God's power; second, I had a sadistic desire, being a young minister myself, to unmask faith healers. If this sounds strange, keep in mind that at the age of 27, I not only considered myself a mature minister, but also one who was totally (or at least liked others to think) commited to the fact that my life was at the disposal of God's power.

But I had to face up to the fact that I never did heal the sick, or raise the dead. Oh, occasionally I went to the hospital when I was a pastor, stood by some dying saint's bedside and prayed, "dear Lord, you know Mrs. Jones loves you; and you know she needs your help; and if it be Thy will, and if there is any way it can be done, please help her. And, dear Lord, if she is not cured, help her to know that You love her anyway and that soon (when she dies) she will be with You forevermore."

You might say that prayer had sufficient protective clauses. The truth is, I never even considered, during all my years of pastoring, and during all my years of evangelism, the possibility of calling people to the front of an auditorium in front of God and everybody, and trying to heal them right there on the spot.

During all this time, I firmly believed that God could do anything He wanted to. And I had, and still have, certain reasons for believing that it is not always to God's or redemption's best interest that every single person be healed of every single physical or mental malady that befalls them. And some of the questions I have along this line I have put to Vic, and his answers will unfold later in the book.

But there was always something else in the back of my mind. It has always lingered there. What if I never did choose a path such as Vic simply because I was too lazy or frankly lacking in spiritual depth?

I'm not going to turn this into a confessional, because I do not feel guilty. What I feel is curious. I've always wondered what kind of person it took, or what kind of power from God, if you will, to stand up there before hundreds or thousands of people, night after night, and stake your entire reputation as a servant of God on whether enough of the people present could be made to believe that what they were seeing were miracles straight from God, no ifs or maybes, or "later on, Mrs. Jones."

This impresses me. We will get into theology, psychology, medicine, and other subjects later. I'm impressed with this guy who stands up there, not once or twice, but night after night, week after week, and takes on deafness, blindness, short legs, cancer, and broken bones with all the grace and confidence of a person who knows a secret and has decided to share it.

I asked Vic about this, and I'll tell you why. After I met with him that night in Wichita, I became a consultant to his ministry. I am president of a computer company called *Church Systems*. I began helping Vic with his mail.

No, I don't read his letters; no, I don't write his letters. I know this is the type thing people like to believe, but it simply isn't true. Vic reads his own mail. He also prepares every response. After he has done this, we take over the responsibility of getting his message on paper and into the mail.

At any rate, it became necessary for me to continue dropping in on Vic's crusades. One of the things that impressed me most is that it is extremely difficult to see Vic during the day when he is in a crusade. I was on my way one week from Houston to San Antonio. Vic was there in a crusade. He knew I was coming to meet with him. I left Houston early Monday morning. I missed the flight direct to San Antonio, and caught a flight to Dallas, ran for a flight to San Antonio, grabbed a taxi and raced for the motel where Vic was staying.

I arrived at the motel at 1:00 P.M. I had missed Vic by twenty minutes. He had already gone to his room. He had left word for me that I could see him that night after the service. All my rushing went down the drain. I had an afternoon in San Antonio to kill.

Vic's reason for this was very simple. Every day that he is in a crusade, he takes care of office requirements in the morning. He then goes to lunch. After this, he goes to his room and spends the rest of the time in prayer until the service that night. He lets nothing interfere with this. He says he has learned that if he makes any exceptions at all, soon there will always be something or someone to take him away from these hours in prayer.

This impresses me. Frankly, I was glad that Vic wouldn't see me. It was extremely refreshing to me; and also reassuring. The man was paying a price for what he was doing. I have never known many ministers who paid a price. If I decided tomorrow to hold a convention for all the ministers I have known who truly had built their ministries on prayer, discipline, and sacrifice and if I had to schedule a place to hold the convention, I would pick out a centrally located phone booth.

Oh, I have known a lot of ministers who reserved the afternoon from public commitments, myself included. But the schedule usually included sleep, the telephone, or the company of a close friend. But consistent daily prolonged periods of prayer is practically a lost art among preachers.

Here's how I put the question to Vic:

"We assume, Vic, that all preachers pray, and that all preachers have to make certain sacrifices in order to be ministers. But this ministry you have entered into is a little beyond what I have known personally. What are the demands?"

"I think," Vic responded, "whenever a man accepts

a responsibility—whether it be executive, school teacher, or politician—there is always a demand. I happen to think that the demand on a minister is much greater.

"Let me take the story back some years. There was a man who had a great influence on my life. He is dead today. His name was Russell West. Russell was the preacher at a camp I attended in 1966. He preached on prayer morning, noon and night.

"Russell West was a man who lived in prayer, he breathed prayer and talked prayer. He preached one day on the three realms of prayer. He used Matthew 7:7, 'ask and ye shall receive, seek and ye shall find, knock and it shall be opened unto you.'

He talked first about the asking realm. He said that's the area most Christians are in; the immature baby stage, where we ask, ask, ask.

"Then he talked of the seeking realm, and finally the ultimate, which was the knocking realm. He said that this was the most intimate area where one could boldly knock on God's door. This man literally caught me up with a thirst for prayer. One afternoon he preached on prayer with such an anointing that it drove me to my knees; I mean literally! I crawled on my hands and knees all the way from the back of the tabernacle to the altar and I stayed on my knees in that same spot throughout the afternoon until time for the service that night. I couldn't stop praying. Instead of staying for the service I went down into the woods and continued praying.

"I was carrying a heavy burden of prayer, and I didn't even think Russell West knew who I was. One day he walked up to me and said, 'Son, I have watched you pray every day. You come earlier and stay longer than anyone else!' For the next two hours he talked with me about prayer. No man ever influenced my life like this man did in those two hours.

"He told me that sometimes it would take months to get into the knocking realm of prayer, and then it could be lost in a week. He said, 'guard it with your life—the knocking realm. It's like an athlete who loses the muscle tone in his body. He has to work twice as hard to build those muscles back.'

"All this really spoke to me. I began to read books like, *Power of Prayer* by E. M. Downs, and *In The School of Prayer* by Andrew Murray. I would read books on prayer and then I would pray. I have never relented in my conviction on prayer.

"In fact, when I first got married, my prayer life bewildered my wife. There were times when I was up before dawn praying. Then, at night when Faye was in bed, I would continue praying 'til after midnight.

"For two and a half years, Faye traveled with me in evangelism. She can attest to the schedule I kept. I would get up every morning at 7:30 A.M., go into the church and study and pray until noon. I came home exactly and methodically at 12:00 noon, had my lunch and spent about thirty minutes with my wife. By 1:00 P.M., I was back in the church and I stayed there praying until 5:00 P.M. I would come home, shower and shave, and return for the evening service. And that was my routine seven days a week. We didn't have nights off in our crusades then. And for over two years at the beginning of our marriage, that was my schedule every single day.

"I have had some preachers ask me why I don't pray for the sick. Very seldom in my services do I pray for people to be healed. I lay my hand on them and command them to be healed. I usually say, 'By the authority of the Name of Jesus Christ, I command you to be healed.' It is more of a command than a prayer. And preachers have asked me about this. I tell them that I do my praying before I get to the service. By the time I get to the auditorium, my soul is running over with prayer.

"If you keep your life spiritually attuned with God, filled with His Word, and with His Faith, then prayer is not a necessity. Jesus did not pray for the sick. The apostles did not pray for the sick. One time Simon Peter found a man lame by a gate. He did not go through a lengthy prayer for the man. Rather, he grabbed him by the hand and said, 'In the name of Jesus Christ, rise up and walk.' Then Peter pulled the man to his feet. That's faith in action. And that kind of strong faith must be backed by strong prayer.

"I know the value of prayer. My team knows that in my crusades, I have certain times that I'll do my business, but there are other times of the day when I feel in my soul a compulsion to pray.

"My prayer life is selfish, because I know you only get what you pay for. I have tried to preach crusades without strong prayer; I have tried to heal the sick in Jesus' name without strong prayer, and my success in such instances is limited. But only when my soul is filled with the blazing confidence of prayer can I really command the blind to see and the deaf to hear.

"I've never liked to glamorize certain sensations that I have when I pray for the sick, because when you do, people begin to feel that's the norm, and if they are to have success in healing, they must also feel the same things. For instance, I was praying one afternoon before a crusade and an unusual and very electrifying anointing of God's Spirit came on the right side of my body. I was numb and cold on my left side, but my right side felt like liquid fire. I lay on my back in this hotel room. I was in the State of Washington, at the time. I had never felt anything like this in my life. Never. My right hand was vibrating. I knew it was the influence of the Holy Spirit.

"I went to the service that night, determined I would tell the people what had happened. When I stepped up to preach, the Spirit of God fell on the audience I gave an altar call and it looked like half the crowd got saved—*and I never preached a sermon!*

"For two weeks, I tried to get my mind on other things, but I could feel this sensation of the Holy Spirit in my right arm. Many times, when I pray for people, not only do I feel a tangible, physical surge of God's spirit, but so do they.

"I have had some of the most conservative, sophisticated individuals one can imagine stand before me and suddenly either melt or explode with emotion. When they try to describe their feelings, they speak of fire or electricity.

"I believe that the spirit of God is a tangible substance that you can feel on your physical form. But I do not believe that faith can be based on what you feel. Faith is based on what you know. Faith comes from knowledge. Faith is like knowing two and two is four. This is a mathematically proven fact. Nobody can tell you that two and two is not four. The things that I know in my ministry are just as settled and concrete in my mind as two and two is four.

"That's why it doesn't shake my faith if a healing sometimes does not happen instantaneously. The Bible says that Jesus Christ had better results in some areas than others. We have the example of Nazareth where Jesus grew up. He went to his own synagogue and tried to preach, but had very little success, because of the unbelief of the people—not Jesus!

"Overall, between 65 percent and 70 percent of those that are healed in my meetings are healed instantly. But there are always 20 percent to 25 percent that go away and are healed progressively.

"Some of the most dramatic miracles of my ministry have not been instantaneous. There was a man named Arthur Stroud who had ten inches of his spine removed by surgery. He was a total paraplegic; could not move his body; confined to a wheelchair. For six years he had been paralyzed.

"The night I prayed for Arthur Stroud, nothing visible happened; not until the next Monday. It was two o'clock in the afternoon when Arthur Stroud got out of his wheelchair and pushed it two blocks down Main Street and into the *Bible Book Store,* testifying to the healing power of God.

"Just across the street was Arthur's pastor who was telling everyone that nothing of value came out of the crusade. The *Bible Book Store* owner walked in and said, 'Have you seen Arthur Stroud?' The pastor said, 'No, where is he?' The owner said, 'He just walked into my store.' The pastor said, 'That's impossible, Arthur's a paraplegic.' The owner said, 'Not anymore; he was healed last night in Vic Coburn's crusade.'

"That has been three years ago and I have documentation that Arthur Stroud is still healed. In this kind of ministry, you cannot let circumstances that sometimes occur affect your faith."

CHAPTER VI

"It Takes Guts"

When I was sixteen two young ministers came to town. One was introduced as a genius and national debate champion. His name was Charles Wellborn. Another was introduced as "God's Groceryman." He was a millionaire. His name was Howard Butt. Billy Graham used to say Howard could outpreach him any day of the week.

At any rate, these two young men swept me off my feet. As I sat listening to them preach, I not only saw them as super preachers, but as super persons! I don't think I doubted, even from the beginning, that I could someday be as good at public speaking as they. But what worried me was their spiritual life. They talked about God, and prayer, and fellowship, and His will in such knowing and ultimate ways. I thought of them as "spiritually deep."

The years passed and I became just as famous and popular a preacher as these two men. (Sounds very brash—but I'm trying to make a point.) In time, there were other young men being influenced by me. And occasionally word would drift back to me that I was considered to be not only a great preacher (ho-hum) but *spiritually deep.*

Comes the confession: I never felt spiritually deep!

I mean, to this day I have never *felt anything!* No electricity; no burning sensation; nothing in either arm; no closeness. Nothing.

I do not question any other man's experience; I simply state my own.

I have stated previously that Vic Coburn impresses me today just as Charlie and Howard did when I was very young. I think of Vic Coburn as being spiritually deep. Even though I no longer think of Howard and Charlie in that way anymore. I no longer think they were really what they appeared to me to be when I first met them. To me they are just a couple of guys who, like me, learned to use the religious lingo early in life, and wound up making their living at it.

Howard has always had, for me, many hang-ups mingled with his spiritual depth. Charlie, I later learned, never really thought of himself as being spiritually deep.

But Vic Coburn sees himself as being "spiritually deep"—close to God—in tune—in touch—however you want to say it. And, as I have already said, I concede that a man who is involved in a faith healing ministry has something that I don't have and never did have.

What is it?

I put this question to Vic and his answer both caught me by surprise, intrigued me and gave me faith in the basic honesty and openness of this man. My question was as follows:

"Vic, when someone sees you today in large crusades and nation-wide television—not merely a prominent minister, but one who has moved to the very front— people would like to ask, 'Why you? What do you have that is distinct? Is it a price you are paying that few other ministers are willing to pay? Did you ever as you were growing up, look at Billy Graham or Oral Roberts and say, "I can do that?" Why Vic Coburn?' "

Here was his reply:

"Let me answer your last question first. No, I never saw Billy Graham or Oral Roberts. I did not have contact with religious circles, nor did my parents.

"As to your first question, I have asked it probably more than any man on earth. 'Why me?'

"There is an experience that I have said little about. It happened a year ago this September (1974). I was in Scotts Bluff, Nebraska in a Holiday Inn, down on my knees searching my heart. I knew God wanted me to launch a nationwide television ministry and I knew both the demands and the responsibility that would follow.

"I was on my knees between two chairs. I desperately wanted to know why God was pointing this out to me. Suddenly I had a deep impression that I should turn on the lamp and read from the New Testament. I did not know what scripture. I flipped on the lamp while still on my knees and opened my Bible. I began reading where Jesus said, 'Ye have not chosen me but I have chosen you and have ordained that you might bring forth fruit and that your trust might remain.'

"I closed the Bible and wept because God had answered my prayer. Certainly I did not deserve to be chosen. The ways of God are strange at this point. Why did God call Saul of Tarsus, the persecutor of Christians? Christ chose this man who called himself the 'Chief of Sinners' for a simple reason:

'He is going to be a witness for My gospel and My sake.'

"I do think God sometimes capitalizes on a person's natural ability. When I look back on my life, I guess I've always been a very gutsy, daring person. I think

God recycled these characteristics and put them into my ministry.

"It takes as much guts to heal the sick as it does faith. Guts may be a crude term, but believe me, to step out before several thousand people and know that every set of eyes is on you; and to know that 30 percent of that audience is skeptical; and they are out there challenging you to do something they don't think you can do.

"You know you can do it through the power of God. But you also know those drilling eyes of scrutiny are straining to see every false move you might make.

"Yes, I have had to have some guts and gall to step out before an audience like that and challenge a blind eye to come open or a cancer to be cured.

"I call this faith, but at the same time, I call it guts, and I'll tell you why. There are a lot of men who have great faith in the theology of healing. They can give you every scripture on the subject. But they are not out there on television, or in a crusade before thousands of people having a skeptic come forward to examine somebody's leg that was two inches shorter than the other.

"I had a woman with a two and a half–inch short leg. I called for a skeptic. A big old brute came forward and said, 'If you are really doing this—if God is in it— then let me push on the leg. If God lengthens it while I'm pushing on it, I'll believe.'

"He pushed so hard he made the woman wrench in pain. I said, 'I'm not even going to touch her legs. You push and I'll pray.

"I began to pray and the power of God lengthened that leg. The man fell on his knees weeping and begging me to forgive him for his unbelief.

"It is a lot like boxing. I boxed in the Golden

Gloves, and you have to psyche your opponent. You may be scared to death, but you have to make him believe that if he dares fight you, you are going to knock his block off.

"I do the same thing sometimes with impossible things. I psyche my people out. I make them believe that I believe what I know I believe, and I never give them a reasonable doubt that I don't believe what I'm preaching, because I do. I think maybe that's a quality about my ministry that has enabled me to demand such faith from people. They see a faith in me that they don't see in possibly anyone else they know.

"Actually, what they are doing is not having faith in their faith, but mine. Many times I've had people say, 'My faith is weak, but if you pray for me, I know I'll be healed.' They have great faith in my faith. In the same way, I have great faith in Christ's faith. They have faith in mine, and I have faith in His.

"People have to have someone to look to who can instill confidence. For instance, I walk, on occasions, through invalid sections that gather around our crusades. I have walked into a room with as many as 150 people sitting in wheelchairs. These people not only have their bodies, but also their faith in a wheelchair. They are in wheelchairs both physically and spiritually. These people are so low that they have given up long ago the idea of ever being well again. When I walk into the room, their heads are down in defeat. Before I walk into the room, I always pray the same prayer: 'God, when I walk into that room, change the atmosphere.'

"I go into the room and immediately command everyone to look at me. And, as they begin to lift their heads and look, you can both see and feel the change in the atmosphere. Why? Because someone is walking in with authority to take dominion over that thing that they cannot take dominion over themselves. I'm not walking in there to pat them on the head and sympathize with them, and give all kinds of false excuses about why they are suffering, and why they have to bear with God, and learn patience, and die for the glory of God. Instead, I say, 'Look, if Jesus Christ were to walk into this room, He would say, 'I'm going to heal you today if you will believe me.' Then, I ask, 'Could you believe Him?'

"When they respond affirmatively, I say, 'Well, He is not here, but I am here, but I am here as His ambassador, and He is going to back everything I do. And when I lay my hand on you in His Name, it's going to be just as though He laid His Hand on you.'

"This is when the collective attitude of the room truly begins to change, and those poor defeated people start looking up. You see, I *know* what God says is true. I have confidence that those words that God spoke to me several years ago are still valid: 'I'm with thee.' If He's with me, if the Name of Jesus Christ has not lost its power, if the Word of God is still valid; if God's compassion is still real—then miracles still happen and must happen when you demand them to happen in faith . . . but it still takes guts."

CHAPTER VII

"How Did He Know That?"

I mentioned earlier in this writing that for a one year period in the late fifties, I became a "Healing Revival Tramp." In order to put together research for a paper at the seminary, I spent dozens of evenings in faith healing revival services.

One of the things that both dismayed and angered me was the cheap, low-road-way that faith healers would go about selecting the persons to be prayed for in the main service. The victims would be asked to come by during the day and fill out a card telling where they hurt and how long. They were given a card and told they would need to return each night until their card came up. This approach served a number of purposes. It built the crowd each night as well as the offering. Primarily, it gave the healer a chance to select the most easily helped and believable candidates.

Those who stood the best chance for their "pre-coded" cards to be chosen were those who had internal, mental, emotional, or physical problems that couldn't be seen with the naked eye; or those who could walk without their crutches but just didn't like to put out the energy or stand the pain. The real toughies were shunted into the darkness night after night, and finally handled in a massive group healing off stage, usually the afternoon before the final night.

In the early stages of faith healing on television, one healer remarked that it usually took careful editing of a dozen services to put together one thirty-minute television service.

Careful scrutiny revealed not only the small number prayed for in proportion to those seeking help, but how much planning it took to get the right people on stage each night. Let me clarify this:

The various kinds of sickness can be placed in four categories:

1. Structural abnormalities, such as cleft palates, hair lips, short limbs.
2. Organic diseases, such as tuberculosis, cancer, diabetes, and stomach ulcers.
3. Mental diseases, such as insanity, or feeblemindedness.
4. Functional disturbances, such as phobias, obsessions, emotionally-induced paralyses, and various forms of hysterical pains.

Most of the healers I observed in my tramping days almost always made their claims for healing in the area of category number two—the organic disorders. However, when all the dust had settled, those who had sustained any apparent healing were from category number four—functional disturbances.

Now, the reason the healer chose organic disorders was obvious. First, this sounded more physical and more dreaded than the others. Second, who can see a cancer go away inside a stomach from the tenth row of a large tent?

The first service I attended of Vic Coburn (the one in Kansas), three things were predominantly different from my tramping days. First, Vic tackled short legs first! Second, before the crusade was over he ultimately prayed for every person present who desired to get up and come to the stage. Third, at times he would go into the audience and point out certain people at random and tell them what was wrong with them before praying for them.

On one occasion, after calling a group to the stage, Vic pointed to a man in the audience and said, "Sir, you have had a strained back for six months. Why didn't you come up on the stage?"

This was so spooky that I had to believe that there were plants in the audience. I had to surrender this viewpoint when Vic visited my hometown of Houston, and I had a chance to see this type thing take place every night. I knew of Vic's schedule and was aware of his seclusion, being cut off even from the phone. Vic would arrive each night after the service had begun. There was no way he could either establish contact with people or learn facts about those present. Yet, he would, on some nights, tell fifty people or more their predicaments with explicit details.

I would be willing to bet you my life that this was no put up job. In all fairness, however, I must tell you that for some reason it is easier for me to believe that a person is clairvoyant than to believe that he is being given insight from God.

Vic calls this procedure "word of knowledge." I asked him about this.

"Vic, you have talked about something called the 'word of knowledge.' You not only command that people be healed, but you apparently are aware of people's needs in advance. Instead of letting people tell you what is wrong with them, on occasions you let them know that you already know what is wrong. When I see someone standing there anxiously shaking their head affirmatively, I am not only impressed, but I find myself wondering if this were not possibly a power, or ability which you had to some degree before you ever thought of becoming a Christian. As a young boy, prior to your religious experience, did you have this inherent power to read people?

"No. That's about as plain as I can put it. I have already told you that the very first time anything like this ever happened to me was two weeks after I had been filled with the Spirit.

"Now, I had received a vision about three weeks before I left the Southern Baptist ministry. I saw a vision of myself. I didn't know who it was. I've only had three of these visions and this same one happened twice. I had the other vision about three years later of Hell.

"But this one regarding me first took place before I was even in the ministry. I saw myself standing in a stadium. I had one of these big walk-on platforms like the one they use for Miss America. I was sitting up in the top balcony and I saw this young man in a black suit preaching to this great mass of people. I thought, 'What is all of this?' Then I focused in on the young man and it was me. This was before I became a minister. Then I had it again right after I received the baptism of the Holy Spirit.

"That was the closest thing I had to the 'word of knowledge' until that night in the service when God told me about the man in the back row with a bad back.

"This experience scared me so much that I actually tried to ignore it for almost two years. Finally, I just relaxed and let the Holy Spirit begin to guide me. One night in Hayward, California, I just let go. God was showing me people who had sicknesses in the service, and I was calling them out, and, sure enough, they were there!

"But one night I missed it. I called for a lady who had a kidney infection. I pointed right to her and there was a lady who responded and came forward. I got her up there and she embarrassed me. She said she didn't have a kidney infection; that her kidney was perfect. This really shook me up. The only thing that kind of saved me was the lady sitting right behind this one stood up and said she had a serious kidney infection and wanted to be healed—so God healed her.

"But I went home defeated that night and I said I wasn't going to do that any more. In fact, I prayed and told God to take this ability away from me. I actually prayed, 'Lord, don't talk to me anymore like that.'

"I went to the service that night and the place was packed. I walked in the front door. I couldn't go in the back door. They didn't have a back door. I had to go down the left aisle up to the platform. I came in late like I always do. The last thing I said before I went in that church was, 'God, don't talk to me about that tonight. I'll preach and I'll get people saved and I'll even pray for the sick. But that's all.'

"Believe me, it's a scary ministry because you're on a very fine line between success and failure and nobody knows the pressure that you're under when you're ministering the 'word of knowledge.' I walked in that church and never even glanced to my left. I walked in and all of a sudden, the voice of God said, 'There's a woman with red hair to your left.' He told me what she had on and said she had perforated ulcers. 'I want you to call her up and I'll heal her.' I went to the platform. I didn't even look. I just turned around with my head down and put my hand over my eyes and I wouldn't even look and I said, 'God, I told You, don't talk to me like that.' And I meant it, I was serious. And do you know what the Holy Spirit said? He said, 'I won't anoint you to preach until you call her up.'

"I looked between my fingers and, sure enough, there she sat out there with red hair, right next to the aisle. I stepped up to the platform and said, 'Well, I'm not going to go ahead and tell you the whole story, folks, but God spoke to me tonight and I wanted to disobey Him, but I can't. I'm going to have to do what He told me to do.' I pointed to this lady and I said, 'Ma'am, I don't know who you are, but you have a serious perforation of ulcers in your stomach.' And she let out a scream, 'Oh, my God' or something like that and she came to the front and sure enough, her stomach was completely perforated with ulcers. She played a trumpet and the doctor told her not to ever blow the trumpet again because if she ever did put any excess pressure on her abdomen, she'd burst whatever was there. But God healed her that night.

"The Lord taught me something that night. It's not what I say; it's what He says. I've never majored in a 'word of knowledge' ministry. There have been times when I could have stepped up in a service and spent two hours just walking up and down the aisles ministering when I had the anointing of the 'word of knowledge' on me so strong. There are times that it's almost like mind reading. I've been sitting with some of my staff members and before they ever said a word, I told them exactly what they were going to say. Now, you can call that mind reading, but it's only been times when I've been very deep in spiritual thought and it seemed like my spirit was taking precedence over my body.

"This happened coming back from a crusade recently. I was reading a book, a spiritual book, and I was thrilled. I turned to Chuck, my organist, and I told him two or three things that he was thinking and it astounded him. The main thing is giving the definition. You see, everything that is functional in the man of God's life must have a purpose. You asked me the purpose of the gift of the 'word of knowledge.' I would say it's the same purpose that the prophets of old had when they could foretell events. It confirmed God's validity. It confirmed God's authenticity. Oftimes, when I can tell sick persons what's wrong with them before they ever tell me, it builds great faith in their hearts. It also brings a tremendous confirmation to others' hearts that God still speaks.

"There is one thing that I think probably should distinguish this ministry from possibly other ministries in years gone by. The Bible says, 'By the hands of the apostles great miracles were wrought among the people and multitudes both of men and women were added on to the Lord daily.' You see, nothing confirms Christ and the gospel like a sign or a wonder or a miracle. We've always tried to equate His sign or wonder or miracle with fanaticism or emotionalism or some weird false doctrine. A sign is like the 'word of knowledge.' That's a sign both to the unbeliever and to the believer that God is there. God is speaking. God knows about those people. A wonder! I think many things can be a wonder. Knowledge can be a wonder. Prophecy can be a wonder. Or even a miracle can be a wonder.

"I think anytime you see a crippled arm straightened and lengthened, that's a wonder. Or a deaf mute healed; that's a wonder. A miracle! Of course, that's something creative; something instantaneous. I think that our ministry combines the gifts of miracles, the gift of faith, the gift of healing, the gift of prophecy, and the gift of 'word of knowledge.' At times, I guess almost every gift of the Holy Spirit functions through this ministry. I don't claim any particular gift. I just praise God for them because they're always working for a purpose: for the edification and the deliverance of individuals."

CHAPTER VIII

"A Short Leg Is a Short Leg
and
A Saved Soul Is a Saved Soul
or
'Creative Miracles'
Plus Evangelism"

Since the seventh inning is recognized as the "stretch" inning in baseball, allow me to pause after seven chapters and review the direction I am taking in this book.

When I was the minister of The First Baptist Church of Tallahassee, Florida, we conducted a most interesting weekly series involving people of various other faiths. One week we would highlight Seventh Day Adventists; the next, Jehovah's Witnesses; the next, Christian Scientists; the next, Mormons, and so on.

Each week I would invite representatives of the faith being highlighted to come as our guests. I always followed the same format: First, I would allow our guests to state their own cases, in their own words. During this time, I would ask leading questions—the kind designed to draw out the clearest and best interpretation of that particular faith. Second, I would ask some very direct questions regarding areas of that particular faith that disturbed me and, I was quite sure, also disturbed many other people.

Finally, I would allow the guests to have the last word. Then we would adjourn. It was not my purpose, either to debate with, or in any way embarrass another person. My sole aim was to enlighten those present with regard to an area that might not be completely clear to them. I felt that it never hurt for people to have a better understanding of those who may think or believe differently from themselves.

I am seeking to follow this same format in this writing. By consenting to cooperate with me in the production of this book, Vic Coburn, in a sense, became my guest. I happen to know he has never before consented to the kind of intensive interviews that were necessary to get this book off the ground.

As my guest, Vic will receive the best and fairest possible hearing I can give. Many times in our interviews, I purposely led him, not to try to trap him, but to give him a chance to lend his best insight concerning certain subjects which I believe many people are anxious to know more about.

As this writing continues, I will present to Vic certain questions which have truly disturbed me. As you will see, Vic will then be allowed to respond in exactly the way he chooses, and we will leave the matter at that. This is neither an expose, nor a debate. Rather it is an exercise in understanding.

In the previous chapter, Vic alluded to what he calls, "creative miracles." These are miracles of a physical nature which are clearly evident; namely, deafness, blindness, or short limbs.

If I am not careful at this point, the reader will be

left with the impression that healing is the only emphasis in a ministry such as Vic's. This is not true. The fact is, that the most impressive thing about Vic's crusade is not the number of people who are healed, but the large number of people who come forward to be converted.

Therefore, I questioned Vic in the following way:

"You mentioned 'creative miracles'. Did you see some sort of development in your ministry along these lines?

"Yes, development is a good word to use. There is no mystery to spiritual growth. Take Billy Graham, for instance. He wasn't always Billy Graham, the acclaimed evangelist. It took time, growth, and study. It took development, hard knocks, and even failure.

"Similarly, I would not be honest if I did not say there have been times of deep doubt and discouragement in my ministry. I think one of the reasons, as I stated earlier, was that I had no standard to go by. I had no Oral Roberts to pattern myself after. It's like passing a course without using the textbook, or having a football team without having ever seen anyone else play the game. Instead, you have men who have been successful in these positions and you study their techniques. You study their training schedule. You study their diet. You study everything about them so that you can pattern after their success.

I think we are a composition of our parents, teachers, and friends; people who have had great influence in our life. I didn't have anyone I could pattern after so I began to just build a pattern myself. I tried to be me. In fact, without sounding egotistical, if I can attribute one thing to my success today, I could peck it out on a piano: 'Be yourself, be yourself, be yourself.' And that's the only kind of person God can use. Someone who is exactly what he is without any pretense; just does what God calls him to do.

"I often like to refer to the growth of my own Christian life and ministry in this way: I refer to the scripture where Jesus said in John's gospel, fifteenth chapter, 'Every branch in me that bringeth forth fruit, my Father will prune it that it might bring forth more fruit.' Any citrus farmer will tell you that unless he prunes his trees, or any grape farmer unless he prunes his vines, he won't have a stronger, heavier crop the following year. I've watched my own ministry and life through the years, especially during the first three or four years of my healing ministry. Almost without fail, every six months I reached a crisis in my life. It was almost like I had to go through some birth pains or something, but I received fresh revelation, fresh understanding. Things that seemed so complicated became elementary to me. Things that were a struggle, became so simple to me. This process I used to call, 'God's purging' and I knew in my heart that God was purging me every so often that I might have a new insight, a new revelation, a new understanding.

"I was talking recently with a friend. I made the confession to her that I am astounded at my ministry. Today, I have more faith than I have ever had in my life. I have the most confident relationship with God I have ever had before in my life. I'm seeing greater miracles than I ever have. It's only been a year or so since I have seen the consistency in cripples as I'm seeing today. I've never seen as many wheelchair cases healed like I have in the last year and a half. I've never seen as many deaf mutes. I've always seen hundreds of deaf people, but there seems to be a greater anointing in the last twelve months. Therefore, all I can do is acknowledge the fact that God is not through purging this ministry.

"Also, in the past two years, I've had a greater ability to win souls; a greater anointing of God to win souls. We've seen 65 percent of our audience accept Christ in one service. There is almost an unbelievable sense of anointing, conviction, and conversion in our services. I consider spiritual power more relevant when it comes to soul winning than I do in divine healing.

"God's gift of healing in my life is a very functional thing. It works day or night with my children, with my own body, with anybody I'm around. Yesterday I walked into this man's office to conduct a business transaction and he was dying with a headache; his back was hurting; his neck was hurting. He said he thought he was going to faint. He said, 'Do you know anything I can take for this terrible headache?' I said, 'Have you ever tried prayer?' He gave me a strange look and said, 'Oh yeah, I'm trying that, too.' I said, 'I guarantee God heals people.'

There were three or four other men in the office and I said, 'Would you let me pray for you?' I said, 'Alright, do you believe in Jesus, healing the sick? Well, He does. By the authority of Jesus' name, I command that headache to be healed.' I laid my hands on him and all of a sudden, the power of God flashed through him and he instantly broke out in a cold sweat. He lost his headache.

"So you see, this gift of healing is not something I use in crusades to bring crowds. It is an ever present thing. It is as natural to me as walking on my two legs."

Let me punctuate something in Vic's statement that he brushed over very quickly. Vic Coburn sees a greater percentage of conversions in his crusades than any other evangelist, including Billy Graham. One cannot attend Vic's services and think that Vic highlights healing above everything else. As we have stated, when he does approach healing, he takes a much more daring posture than is normal for most faith healers.

But the first thing Vic does in every crusade service is preach an evangelistic sermon. In fact, some nights he does not approach the matter of divine healing at all. However, there is never a service when he does not seek to reach the lost for Christ.

If the proof of a ministry is in the results; and if one looks for the most tangible possible results in the area of healing; and if one looks to the number of people who accept Christ—then there appears to be a great deal of proof in Vic's ministry.

CHAPTER IX

"What to do
When the Doctor Leaves"

One can hardly look through the past century at the progress of medicine without catching his breath: the internal organs threatening life that have been removed; the stomach has been opened; the whole of the intestines have been removed and replaced; one half of the brain has been removed; the human heart has been entered with the surgeon's knife.

I have been keenly interested through the years in the various attitudes held toward medical science by faith healing groups. It would certainly not be fair to say that all faith healing groups frown upon medicine with the same vehemence as, for instance, the Christian Science Movement.

Some faith healers look upon doctors as necessary evils who are to take care of people who do not have the faith and good sense to trust God.

Other healers see doctors as a luxury afforded the rich, whereas God has provided for the poor a better means of healing that would be available to all, rich or poor.

Many faith healers are quick to concede that medical men have knowledge, and even much knowledge. They simply desire to point out that there is a higher knowledge of God available for men which involves the healing of the sick.

THE DOCTOR'S DAY IN COURT

Before we hear what Vic thinks about the doctors, let's hear what the doctors think about Vic, or at least men in his field of endeavor.

One thing that bothers the doctors is the scarcity of case histories accompanying a person who desires healing. The doctor feels that no layman (non-medical person) is qualified to diagnose his sickness, much less determine whether he is healed; and certainly, they think, public testimonials of healings at moments of great excitement and emotional stress are worthless.

Many of these doctors claim they know what they are talking about. They claim they are often called to serve the same people for the very same disease of which they were supposed to have been cured by the faith healer.

Other doctors do not question that some people are, in fact, cured, or healed. What they question is whether there was anything "miraculous" about the healing, any more than when a person is healed by the drugs they prescribe.

Also, there are some doctors who get extremely perturbed over the fact that most faith healers will claim no responsibility for failures. The blame is always thrown back on the patient. Jesus one day told his disciples that they could not heal a little boy because their faith wasn't strong enough. Modern-day doctors feel they have a hard time finding a faith healer who would accept such a rebuke, even from Christ himself.

Probably the strongest point of contention for men of medicine is the practice among faith healers of ignoring proven remedies. In the first place, it has never appeared that God made a practice of helping people where they can help themselves. In the second place, doctors see death as a poor way to prove a point. A decade ago, a famous faith healer in the South lay for three weeks without medical assistance, only to be taken finally to the hospital when it was too late. The doctors present shrugged and said they could have helped him if they had gotten to him sooner.

Then there are some doctors, who are also Christians, who get pretty mad at the idea that they work in the natural realm while the faith healer works in the spiritual realm. For instance, we no longer have any real problem with polio. Doctors ask, "Was this really all Professor Salk and no part God?" "Why is it," many doctors ask, "that God so quickly honors the public prayer of a Christian faith healer, but ignores the private but diligent search of a Christian doctor?"

VIC AND THE DOCTORS

While attending Vic Coburn's crusade services, I heard the evangelist use a particular phrase when praying for some people who had an apparently crucial internal disorder. He would not pass off the matter lightly. He would, instead, say to the individual, "Go back to your doctor tomorrow and see if things aren't different."

When we had a chance to pursue this matter of the medical field, I posed serveral questions:

C. A.: "Vic, how do you see your role? Are you a co-worker with medicine? Are you a substitute for medicine? Do you consider doctors your friends or your enemies? Do you view persons who go to doctors as excercising a lack of faith? What do you see as your role in this matter?"

Vic: "First, let me say that I personally believe that my ministry should complement medical science. I'm not against medicine. I don't fight doctors because I think that anything that helps alleviate suffering humanity has to be a mercy of God. But here you have to differentiate between God's divine and physical healing. Doctors themselves will be the first to confess, if they're honest, that all they do is assist natural recovery.

"If it's God's will that we be sick, why did God go to such extreme calculated planning to program health and healing processes in our body? Even natural healing tells us that God's will is that we be healed; everything—the antibodies and the white and the red corpuscles and all things that God so instituted in our bodies—everything is programmed to fight sickness, fight germs, fight alien forces that would dare infiltrate God's Temple.

"Yes, I believe in medical science. I'm not a preacher of medical science. I don't advocate people who are enlightened to God's Word and enlightened to God's will to place medical science and doctors' care over God's power because I'm a fanatic. I'm a total believer in God's power. I don't take medicine myself. I don't advocate that people don't take medicine.

"I don't say much either way except when a doctor gets on my toes sometimes, I get on his toes. But as far as I'm concerned, many doctors are very reputable, very dedicated. However, some of them are very unscrupulous. It's been proven by the American Medical Association that tens of thousands of unscrupulous unnecessary surgeries are committed every year across America by recognized, licensed medical practicioners. The word practicioner means just what it says. They've been given legal right to practice on you. So, basically, there's nowhere in the legal code of medical conduct that says that doctors have the right to heal anyone.

They're not divine; they're not to be eulogized or idolized by our society. We have done that. We've made movies out of them and our society places them on an abnormally high pedestal.

"The faith healer prays for someone and that patient dies and the healer receives adverse publicity all over the country. But if you'll go down to any doctor in the nation and check his files, you'll find hundreds of case histories where people he treated died, and many of them died even after he pronounced them cured from certain diseases. So, all I'm saying is that I think that my ministry and a ministry of healing should deserve at least the same benefit of doubt as medical science, for we are in the same field of healing. We're just using different methods. Their method is assisting God's natural recovery process that He's computed; programmed in human bodies. My method is invoking God's divine healing power to bring instantaneous and aggressive and miraculous cures."

C. A.: "Let me ask you if this would not be a fair statement. Now, I'm not trying to put words in your mouth. But, have you found it to be true that most people go to doctors with every intention of getting well? In other words, they are pretty convinced of what they have wrong with them and they are going to be able to get rid of it and the doctor is going to help them. But, I get the idea from observing and watching and being in your services, most of the people who come to you don't have any other hope. They've already been the doctor route and when you get them, if you can't help them, they're not going to have anywhere else to go. Is this not true?"

V. C.: "Yes, in fact, you see, I'm under constant attack, scrutiny, and criticism from, not just the medical profession, but from the intellectual society we live in.

"But I want to say this: I wish my critics could read the thousands of letters I get and could stand on platforms of auditoriums across the nation and could listen to the hopeless, pleading pathetic cries of suffering, diseased, afflicted people who come to me that are broke. They have spent their life savings on doctor bills, hospitalization, medication, and they have been operated on from one to fifteen times. And they come up and tell me that since surgery, they are in ten times more pain. They have no money, their body is wracked with more problems than it was before. Then, I think people would understand my point of view more. You see, the doctor every so often hears of a person who went to a faith healing meeting and was prayed for and didn't get healed. So he cries the voice of disapproval that people are being taken advantage of and they are getting their hopes raised falsely.

"Well, I could say the same thing. What about the tens of thousands of people that go to their doctors week after week and lay down hard earned cash with a promise of their doctor that he's going to give them cobalt treatment and cure them of cancer, and he's going to give them cortisone injections and relieve their arthritis. Then, six months later, after he takes their life savings and their insurance policy and their stocks and bonds, he then turns and says, 'There is no hope, nothing more I can do for you.' Then they come to my crusade broke, dying, frustrated, and hopeless and I get them when everybody else is through.'

C. A.: "Sometimes in your meetings you tell people to go back to their doctors or to come back and let you know if they were healed. Do you ever have anybody that you check up on later and you find that they are still doing alright?"

V. C.: "Yes, in fact, every person that now comes

across my platform who is prayed for and apparently receives a healing, we give them a card. One of my staff members fills out the card with their names and addresses. On the back, we write down the doctor's name and address and we send a follow-up letter to these people. Of course, many of them don't respond immediately. I get letters all the time from people who say they were healed two years ago at such and such a meeting but never wrote me a testimony. I go into a city where I haven't visited for a year or two and many people come up saying that they were healed of a deaf ear or a bad leg or stomach ulcer or heart problem, and they are still healed. I am dealing in a mass ministry, not only millions on television, but thousands in crusades. It is impossible with a limited staff and personnel to follow up on everyone who is prayed for. However, I do thoroughly tell my people that God's power can withstand medical scrutiny. 'Go back to the doctor. Let him examine you. And take God's Word with you.' "

CHAPTER X

"Television"

Before we continue with other theological questions which arise from a study of a healing ministry, perhaps we should pause and discuss that media which makes and breaks ministries of this sort every year—television.

Each year the same thing happens to both the just and the unjust—a person will be made into an American legend, within the briefest period of time, simply because of the broad and encompassing scope and power of the T.V. media. Then, this same person can be made into a fool or a bore or a farce or simply dropped into an abyss of nothingness—all because of the explosive, destructive, revealing, corrosive power of the T.V. media.

Many of the persons my company represents have made the decision to involve themselves in a T.V. ministry. I am always curious, usually from a psychological aspect, as to what it is that makes a person want this kind of ministry. To me, a person has to be one step from insanity to walk, with eyes open, into television.

There are, once again to me, only two wholesome reasons for opting for a television ministry: one, the hope that the whole world might be reached for Christ; and two, that the minister might hope to become famous.

The reason I am quick to sympathize with a man who seeks to minister by T.V. is because, once again to me, there can be only two sources for the motivation: God, or stupidity. If it is God, I don't want to buck Him; if the latter, I am always drawn to the underdog.

Why madness? Because T.V. is expensive; so much more expensive than anything else a minister can tackle. Television is expensive for several reasons: first, it demands the use of costly equipment; second, it demands the use of highly technically oriented persons; third, it obviously reaches so many people with its message.

Commercial T.V. is a good deal for the sponsors or originators and a bad deal for the viewers—you and me. A soap company can produce a T.V. program. They can add the cost of the T.V. to the price of the soap. Then, they can put the soap in a store a few blocks from your house and mine. The results are fantastic.

The preacher is in a similar situation when he preaches, and then passes the plate before he lets the people leave the building.

But consider how dreadful would be the plight of the soap company if they had to depend on the viewers to send the price of the soap to the soap company before they (the viewers) even receive their soap.

This is the plight of the T.V. minister. He must pay for all costs of T.V. production, dubbing (copying of tapes), shipping to stations, purchase of air time, publicity, and mail costs telling about the T.V. program—all this before he can hope to realize a cent from any of it. Furthermore, he cannot use the local store. He cannot urge his viewer to go take a gift to the nearest church. The nearest church would simply spend it.

Also the T.V. preacher is prohibited from sounding like he wants money. He has to offer the people watching a gift, or infer he needs their prayers and support, hoping they will read between the lines that "support" means money.

Every man I know who is involved in a T.V. ministry has to go night and day in an effort to pay for this little spoiled brat whose only asset is that he, (the T.V. tube) works his way into the stream of consciousness of four out of every five Americans each year (whether for good or evil will not even be discussed at this time).

From where I sit, something happens to a minister closely akin to getting car fever. You don't think about a new car for years. Then, one day you begin to ponder the idea and you never stop until you have not only looked at every new car around, but rushed headlong into some car dealership and demanded that they work out a way to get you the car of your dream.

I'm not trying to take the divine out of the matter. I'm simply saying that it is difficult for me to see reason behind all the sacrifices and heartaches that a man brings on himself by taking on T.V. from the standpoint of a non-profit perspective.

At this writing, I have been the producer of a weekly T.V. program for over a year. I know what I am talking about. I have enjoyed it because the experience allows me to spread my creative wings while using another man's money, plus being paid. But I must destroy an illusion for you. T.V. is not an easy undertaking for a minister—any minister. No fame, or personal recognition is worth it. And neither the government, nor God's people, nor the greedy T.V. tube will ever allow the minister to be rewarded financially as he deserves.

Still, men do it. And there is no question about the fact that people are reached in ways beyond compare.

The minister whose T.V. I produce, (Bob Harrington) had been preaching for fourteen years before he entered T.V. His first year on television, he preached to more people than all previous fourteen years combined.

VIC COBURN

About six months before his entrance into television, Vic went to Rockford, Illinois, to conduct a crusade. He met a minister named Don Lyon, who was pastor of the large First Church of the Open Bible, who had his own television program called, "Quest for Life." Reverend Lyon had just purchased a mobile television unit and offered to televise one of Vic's crusade services.

Vic had never seen himself on T.V. His initial reaction to the crusade taping was negative. He questioned whether the emotion, feeling, excitement—in short, the anointing of God would come through the video tape.

Finally, Vic consented and the T.V. crew taped the last service of the crusade in full. The two of them, Vic and Reverend Lyon, sat in the van the next day and viewed the footage. They sat weeping. The service had lost nothing in the translation from life to tape. The power of God came through to Vic beyond all he had imagined.

As the two men sat in the truck, Reverend Lyon looked at Vic and said, "I've been healed."

"What do you mean?" Vic didn't know he was sick. He wasn't. He wore contact lens. Sitting there, the minister took them out of his eyes and put them in the pocket.

"I can see."

And he could. The next day Don Lyon took his driving test. All restrictions regarding glasses were removed. He has not worn glasses since the experience in the van.

Don Lyon began to work hard to interest Vic in a T.V. ministry.

"Look, Vic," he would say repeatedly, "America needs your kind of television ministry. At one time, there were a couple of men who did this, but no one today is really showing people the actual power of God in 'living color'. People preach about it; they sing about it; they talk about it; they interview it; they talk to people who have been healed. But no one has a program that you can tune in and see right before your eyes God's healing power. Vic, I believe God is calling you into a nationwide T.V. healing ministry."

Vic kept telling Don that he couldn't do it. He had no experience in television. And he didn't want to tackle something that he knew so little about.

Before the two men parted that day, Don said to Vic, "I'm going to pray that in your sleep you will see millions of T.V. sets."

Vic laughed and told him goodby. He put the idea out of his mind. And it would stay out for a few days, and then return. Soon, the matter began to dominate his thinking enough that he began to pray about it. A seed had been planted in Rockford that was God's beginning and was destined to grow.

He would sit late in the evening and think how he could preach to 5,000 people a night 365 days a year for twenty years and not preach to as many people as he could on one nation-wide telecast. The thought was staggering to him.

Soon, Vic was consumed in thought and prayer about television. He could think of little else. He prayed for weeks about this one single matter: a national T.V. ministry. Then one night it was settled. Vic said to his wife, "God wants us to reach America, and maybe the world, through television."

THE FIRST STEP

The recipe for tiger soup begins with catching a tiger. And a television program begins with catching a television producer. Vic had one of his staff members begin to search out such a person. One name kept popping up in the investigation: Larry Coyle, of the Coyle Advertising Agency. Vic gave him a call.

Larry Coyle happens to be a very dear friend of mine. Vic is fortunate to have him for a producer and Larry is fortunate that Vic Coburn came his way. However, the two men almost missed each other.

When Vic got Larry on the line, he told him who he was and that he was planning a television program. Larry not knowing Vic, told him to get in line. He told him he receives calls all the time from people who want to go on television.

Larry quickly outlined all the obstacles that emanate from a man thinking he should be on T.V. Finally, Vic broke in.

"Look, Mr. Coyle, I'm not asking you if I can go on television. I'm going on television. I just want to know if you're interested. It's going to be one of the greatest television ministries in America. Whoever has my account will see it become the biggest thing in his agency."

Larry decided it would be worth a trip to one of Vic's crusades. He took his wife with him, informing her that he was going to do everything possible not to be impressed.

The opposite occurred. Both Larry and his wife were greatly impressed. They met Vic at the motel after the service. They talked until 4:00 A.M. Vic shared with them the vision he had for the Lord's work. He confessed that he did not know anything about television; and he had no money.

As they continued talking, Larry confided to Vic that he had been praying that God would give him an opportunity to work with a ministry that would magnify the power of God.

Both men agreed that a "Show and Tell" ministry was needed for America: one that would not only preach Christ, but would also demonstrate over T.V. the miracles of God. And Vic knew he was the man to do it.

"If I can just get that camera into that crusade and get away from being self-conscious about the camera, I know enough dynamite is going off in those services to explode faith across America."

That night, the two men agreed on a target date to begin—the following April. They also agreed they would need a quarter of a million dollars to activate the total project. Actually, it was Larry who, from experience, put the figure of a quarter of a million into the picture. Vic had not seen this kind of money in his ministry. However, his ministry had been solvent. He had always paid his bills, met his expenses, and kept a slight reserve in the bank. Larry tried to warn him.

"You must understand, Vic, that television eats up a lot of money. You can spend more money in a couple of months on T.V. than you would in a year of crusades." Vic wouldn't be discouraged.

"Larry, don't worry about it. I know God wants me to do this and that's all that matters."

THE SECOND STEP

In the next few weeks, as planning began for production, practically everyone on Vic's staff was apprehensive about the new venture. One staff member was fired for voicing to the rest of the staff the fact that he thought Vic was making the biggest mistake of his life, trying to launch a nation-wide T.V. program with no money.

All the emotions that ran through Vic's mind during these weeks were perfectly normal. He considered the possibility that he was simply feeding his own ego. He wondered if he had misread God's direction. He stayed on his knees for several days. His conviction only deepened that he was doing the right thing.

Vic began trying to communicate his plans through the mail. It took a while for those on his mailing list to grasp the enormity of what Vic was doing. He was not planning to begin on one or two stations. He was planning to begin all at once—on stations across the nation—and in prime time wherever available.

To this point in his ministry, Vic had never raised any money beyond merely taking an offering in his services. He was now faced with the necessity of getting into fund raising in a big way.

The first taping took place in a crusade in El Paso, Texas. Vic was excited. Larry handed him the bill—$20,000. Vic almost fainted. Still, he did not waiver to those around him. They were still in December of 1973. Their target date was April, 1974.

"Don't worry," Vic told all those around him at El Paso, "we will have everything we need to begin by April."

His words were enough to console those about him, but Vic still did not know how things would fall in place. On the plane home from El Paso, Vic came upon a plan to raise the money needed for the kickoff of T.V. in April. He took a felt pen and wrote his thoughts down. The next day he called his staff together and laid the plan before them.

During the following two months he conducted fifteen Partner's Banquets. Each time he showed a preview of the El Paso taping. By April 1, there were enough funds to begin. The big question still remained, one Vic asked himself often during those days: "Will people watch this kind of program?"

He was counting on one factor: that he had a plot that Hollywood couldn't duplicate. He was not going to air a farce about ministers. He was not going to involve people in a "search for a cure" along the lines of a Jerry Lewis telethon. He had the cure! And he was going to put it before the eyes of all who would choose to see. And it would all be done in good taste.

THE THIRD STEP

The first program was aired publicly in Phoenix, Arizona. It was placed in prime time and aired just before Vic's Phoenix crusade. Immediately following the telecast—in three days—the crusade office recorded over 1,000 phone calls which came as a direct result of this one telecast. More stations were added. The mail began coming in from all over the country. Thousands of letters were received; letters that were filled with thrilling stories of victory, deliverance, and healing.

A seventy-three year old man wrote that he had been an Orthodox Jew all his life. He watched the telecast in Los Angeles and became convinced that Jesus must be the Messiah because of the confirmation of God's work that he witnessed by television. He told Vic that he had accepted Christ as Lord that very day while watching T.V.

Another letter came from a seventy-one year old woman. She knew nothing about faith healing and was very skeptical. She had been in great pain for over three years. Vic had told the viewing audience to touch the television or touch their bodies where they hurt. These were her words:

"I reached over and touched the television. Please don't think I'm a fanatic, but something went through me. I have never felt anything like it. For three days now, I have had no pain. Most of all, something inside my heart has changed."

A sixty-one year old businessman wrote. He lived in Phoenix and owned three hundred acres right in the downtown area. He said, "I've been the dirtiest sinner for twenty years. I have mocked preachers. The other night I watched your telecast. Right there in my living room I fell on my knees and accepted Jesus as my Lord and Saviour."

People often get the impression that a minister on television only asks people to write so they will send money. Those who believe this have short memories and fail to recall the encouragement that a letter can often bring. Listen to Vic:

"Out of the thousands of letters we receive, not a half of a percent are negative. Instead, they are either from positive viewers or from people who ask very positive questions. People write to say that they have been taught prayer all their lives, but this is the first time they have ever seen the power of prayer fulfilled before their eyes.

"Seventy-five percent of our mail comes from non-dedicated church people; people who are unsaved. It is obvious from their letters that they were initially attracted by the healings. But there is always an urgent gospel appeal at the end of every program. Reading the mail is what encourages me to preach Christ as earnestly as I know how."

THE DAY OF MIRACLES

After much prayer, and after discussing over one hundred titles with his wife and Larry Coyle, Vic decided to call his T.V. program "The Day of Miracles." He liked this title because he wanted to remind both himself and his viewers that the ultimate proof of this television venture had to rest in the power of God working today in the lives of people.

In the early programs, Vic experimented with putting the preaching first and the healing last. He found that the television response was not as strong this way even though it was a most effective format for a crusade service. He reasoned this way: people who came to the crusade were already interested. However, many people watching T.V. have made no such commitment. If they see a man preaching at the beginning, this is no different than dozens of other programs available. The result: they turn the dial. But if they see a healing line at the very outset, they become intrigued. This format destroys the indifference of a viewer and prepares him for the sermon to follow.

The matter of format raises the question as to which is the most important: the message of salvation, or physical healing. This will be discussed more fully in a later chapter.

At this writing, Vic Coburn's T.V. ministry is one year old. His program probably draws more raw mail response per viewing audience than any other religious program on T.V.

There are some who think no preachers should be

allowed on T.V. There are others who think that no minister should be allowed to portray alleged healing miracles on television. Such questions must always lead to the ultimate—and only truly relative question—is God working in the world today?

If a person believes God is not working in the world, it is natural that he would resent any and all religious exploitation, either in person or on television. If a person believes that God is working today in the lives of people, then that person is obligated to search out those persons who appear to be authentic and lend them their prayers and support. For what it may be worth, this is Vic's vision for his ministry on television:

"I go into a city—any city—and I cannot be any other place at that time. But, because of television, I'm going into the homes and hearts of countless millions of people every week. My vision is to show all of America that there is a God who works miracles.

"America is going to know that there is at least one preacher who believes in praying the prayer of faith for miracles. The people who write me have desperate needs. I don't blame them for choosing to write me. If I were in deep need, I would write someone who believed God was still in the business of helping people."

An interesting footnote:

After much deliberation, I thought I would go ahead and say that at this writing, Vic Coburn is spending above $140,000 per month to keep "The Day of Miracles" on television. Obviously, many people make great sacrifices to contribute to this endeavor. And I know there are those who will gasp at the above figure and be appalled that such funds are expended in this way.

Let me simply add a footnote which you might find interesting. And I hope as I do that you will not think me naive. From the beginning, I indicated that I had no intent or desire to write a negative critical book about faith healers. I am aware of the many criticisms that have been made and can be made still about some. My desire is to create understanding.

In that vein, let me add a note that is often overlooked. One would be amazed at the number of medical payments insurance companies do not have to pay; the number of medicare payments the government does not have to pay; the money the government does not have to spend in drug rehabilitation—all of these—because of a ministry such as Vic's.

Whether or not God's healing takes place in all these instances is open to debate. That vast amounts of money are saved because people responded to this ministry is a fact.

And by the way, don't ever worry about a minister on television spending the money you send or give him on himself. He is usually keeping everything he owns in hock to stay on the "tube."

CHAPTER XI

"Sickness unto Death (or How Does One Get Out of This World?)"

Did you ever play the game of association? If not, let me explain. Someone says a word or phrase; you respond with the first thing that comes to your mind.

Let's try it: you say, "Faith Healing." Here's what immediately comes to my mind:

1. All sickness and suffering is caused by sin.
2. It is not God's will that anyone be sick.
3. If one will repent of sin and have faith, he/she will be forgiven of all sin and cured of all sickness.

The first of the above three statements is not the sole property of faith healing beliefs. It is more formally called the principle of retribution. Those who incorporate the idea that all sickness and suffering is caused by sin do so by patching together certain passages of scripture from the Old Testament.

To me, this type thinking points up just how dangerous a book the Bible can become when used wrongly or for ulterior purposes. Let me insert, at this point, certain definitions which, though not apparently apropos at this stage, may prove helpful to your thinking as we proceed. A *text* is any particular passage of scripture in the Bible. A *context* is the scripture on both sides of the text. Often the context will encompass an entire chapter, or even an entire book from the Bible. The context helps to clarify why a text was stated, to whom, by whom and when. A *pretext* is what happens whenever a text is taken out of context. We have all suffered from being quoted "out of context." The same thing happens to the Bible everyday.

Exagesis is a word which means "to take out of a passage of scripture that *and only that* which can be supported by the context. *Isogesis* means just the opposite. This is when a person already has certain beliefs or convictions of his own and he goes searching through the Bible for a verse (usually in this case called a proof text) that will support that which he already believes.

Let me summarize. *Exagesis* is what a student of the Bible does when he searches the context before drawing any sweeping conclusions about a particular passage of scripture. *Isogesis* is what happens when a fanatic runs through the Bible grabbing for support from any word or phrase he can find simply because he has had to redouble his effort after he has lost his aim.

My point: to say sin brings suffering and, in some cases, sickness, is not an insupportable premise. But to say that all sickness and suffering is caused by sin almost "boggles my mind beyond repair."

In 1962, I became pastor of The First Baptist Church of Tallahassee, Florida; a church, I would like to take this opportunity to say in print, that was filled with some of the most wonderful people God ever put on the face of the earth. At this writing in 1974 (twelve years after coming to Tallahassee, and seven years after leaving there) I do not recall one person for whom I hold any negative feeling.

The first week I was in Tallahassee, I was on a panel for a student retreat for Florida State University. There was another Baptist minister on the panel that week who was supposed to explain the doctrine of sin. He began with the premise we have already mentioned: "All sickness and suffering is caused by sin."

I challenged him on the point. I used an event that had taken place that very weekend on the lake where we were having the retreat. Eighteen black children—all below the age of seven—had drowned in a row boat that capsized. I asked the minister to explain this event in the light of his premise about sin and suffering. I asked him what these little children could have done to merit this punishment. This was his reply. "We have no way of knowing *what* they had done; but you can be sure that each one had sinned sufficiently in his young life to merit the punishment of God which fell that day on the lake."

This incident reminded me of Albert Camus' book, *The Plague*. As a plague gradually unfolded in the city, a certain minister could not wait to get to his pulpit to explain to his people that the plague was the result of their sin. It was God's judgment, which would be taken away only when the people repented of their sins and turned to Jesus Christ.

The people began to repent in droves, and they continued to die in droves. As time passed, the preacher, while not changing his doctrinal position, became less anxious to enter the pulpit.

A doctor challenged the minister as to why he held so strongly to the premise that *all* sickness had to be the result of sin. He pointed to the case of a sweet young eight–year–old boy who was dying from the plague. The doctor asked, "Why can you not make an exception for this young lad who has done no harm to anyone?"

The preacher replied, "Because one has to believe everything or deny everything. I choose to believe everything."

The boy died. The doctor chose to deny everything rather than strip innocence from the boy. Ultimately, the minister becomes ill. He finally dies. But he does not die from the plague. He dies from losing heart in the attempt at defending an indefensible position in the face of mounting tragedy all around him.

I have a ten year old son. He is a lovely child. If he died tomorrow, I do not know what I would do to the man who tried to tell me sin killed him.

I believe. But I don't believe everything! Nor do I deny everything. I reject easy answers to difficult and perplexing mysteries that track us all through life.

In the rest of this chapter, and in those to follow, I want it understood that this, for me, is no exercise in theory about faith and its relation to healing and to God. This, for me, is an honest and urgent effort to determine what one can and cannot expect from God; and what God does and does not expect from us.

I have no desire on this earth to take one chink from the armor of God, or from God's men. I desperately want to help human beings find a way to glorify God in the context of their own human frailties.

The three premises at the beginning will form the vantage point for other discussions in later chapters. Actually, for this chapter, a two-pronged question emerges. If it is, in fact, God's will that all people be healed; if physical health is that important; and if God is compassionate, and wants everyone to be well—why is it that he has to wait on a Vic Coburn to come along and tell Him to help someone before He does help them? It seems that God would not have to wait on the instruction of a mere human being.

The second part of my question is this: if physical health is this important, how is a person ever going to die without getting old and tired and weak and sick? Is it God's plan that every person be simply caught up in the midst of good health and taken to heaven?

Vic: "You ask why God has to have one like myself to heal the sick if He is so compassionate. Why can't God reach down His Hand and heal people? Ask yourself this: why doesn't God save everyone since He is a compassionate God and the Bible says it is not His will that any should perish? The answer is simple. God does not arbitrarily force His will on any person. He does not go down the street slapping people down with conviction. The Bible says, 'How can they believe in whom they have not heard, and how can they hear without a preacher? And how can they preach unless they be sent?'

"The only way that people come to Jesus Christ is through a preacher, or a witness. No person is ever saved, has ever been saved, without some form of human instrumentality.

"When God wanted a law written, He didn't send an angel down to deliver it; He sent a man up to the mount to write it. God didn't write the Holy Scripture on the sky. Instead, He used men to write His Word to men.

"God has always limited Himself to the limitations of men. Throughout history, God has always operated on the principle of incarnation. God's method has always been a man. He placed the revelation of Himself in a man—Jesus Christ. God's method has always been men: to preach, to witness, to heal. And God has always been limited to the obedience of His servants to go into the world and carry out His commands. As I interpret the Bible, God has no other plan than that those who love Him will carry out His will. This is true both for salvation and for healing.

"Now, let's deal with second part of the question. If it is God's will that people be healed, how can people die? How can they go out of this world in dignity?

"There is no scripture in the Bible that says a person has to die of sickness. The Bible does say that a man is alloted three score and ten years—or approximately seventy years.

"Take the example of Moses, who died when he was one hundred and twenty years old and his eyes were not even dim. He did not die of a disease. He just died. Old age does not have to be culminated by cancer or some other incurable disease. There is such a thing as a man reaching a certain age when he simply dies. This is the kind of death that glorifies God. This is the kind of death that reaches an apex of physical health and dies.

"If one studies the Old Testament, he finds that diseases and physical afflictions were a part of the curse of the law. The Bible says that Jesus Christ became a curse that He might destroy the curse of the law.

"Let's get to the crux of this issue. Is it God's will to heal everyone? First, let me ask a question. Is it God's will to be honest? Is God an honest God? Will God keep His Word? Did He mean what He said? Did He say exactly what He meant? If He did, then there is ample evidence in the Bible that God does want everyone to be healed. Let me cite a few examples. In the fifty-third chapter of Isaiah, referring to the coming of

Christ, it says, 'By His stripes we are healed.' I Peter 2:24 says of the redemptive act of Christ, '. . . took our sins in His own body on the tree that we being dead to sin might live unto righteousness . . . by whose stripes ye were healed!' Either this is unnecessary repitition or it means that provision for both salvation and physical healing were accomplished by Christ on the cross. Listen also to Matthew 8:17: '. . . Himself took our infirmities and bore our sicknesses.' Jesus took our sins. If we also bear them, it's not His fault.

"The Book of Acts is filled with accounts of God's healing compassion through His apostles and disciples. And incidentally, the healing was not confined merely to the apostles of Christ. Philip was not an apostle. Yet, Acts 8 tells of his going to Samaria to preach and 'great miracles were wrought.' Steven was not an apostle. Yet the Bible says he was a man of faith and power who did great miracles among the people.

"James 5:14 says, 'Is any among you sick? Let him call for the elders of the church. Let them pray over him anointing him in oil and the prayer of faith shall save the sick and the Lord shall raise him up.' That passage leaves no room for doubt. The word, 'any' means everyone—no conditions. Of course, the key phrase in this passage is 'the prayer of faith.' This has marked the breakdown of many ministers, theologians, students and other Christian servants today. There are those who say Christ doesn't heal today, when in reality they simply do not, or cannot, or will not, pray the prayer of faith. Instead of confessing their own lack of spiritual power, or confessing their non-belief, they choose rather to try to explain away God's reality.

"Let's look for a moment at the ministry of Jesus Christ. Hebrews 13:8 says, 'Jesus Christ, the same today, yesterday and forever.' That's clear, simple and absolutely positive. It doesn't say there will be a new dispensation where Jesus Christ will lose His power and compassion.

"I know there are those who say that Jesus healed people in order to get His ministry kicked off with a bang; that this was merely a temporary display of God's power along the order of an inauguration. But now that all that's over, God doesn't do that sort of thing. In all the history of man's plight on the earth, God chose to release His healing power and compassion on the human race for three brief years in order to help spotlight His Son.

"To those reading this who would even doubt the fact that Jesus healed people while He was on earth, I have nothing to add. But to those who do, let me ask you a question. Do you really believe that if Jesus were to return to earth today in all His glory—do you think for a moment He would ignore the sick and not heal them?

"Jesus would do the same thing today that He did yesterday; and that He will do forever—heal those who are sick!

"The above 'inauguration argument' simply doesn't hold water, and I'll tell you why. That isn't why He healed people. The Bible tells us that Jesus healed people because He was moved with compassion. Listen to this: a leper comes to Jesus and cries out, 'Lord, if it be your will, heal me.' And the Bible says, 'Jesus was moved with compassion and put forth His Hand and healed him' (Mark 1:40). It doesn't say that Jesus said, 'Hey, this will be a good chance to show these people who I am.' It says He was moved with compassion. Let me ask you this: do you think Jesus Christ is any less compassionate today than He was yesterday? I don't.

"Acts 10:38 says, 'Jesus Christ of Nazareth, anointed by the Holy Ghost in power, went about doing good . . . healing all that were pressed of the devil.' In this passage, the writer actually categorizes physical illness as an oppression of the devil. In other places, the Bible says that great multitudes were brought to Christ and 'they were healed everyone.' They were all healed.

"In other words, Jesus made no exceptions, but healed everyone. Do you think if He made no exceptions yesterday, that He will begin making them now? I don't.

"If sickness came in the first place by the curse of the law, then Jesus Christ, who destroyed the cause of the curse, also destroyed the effect of the curse.

"When a disease is healed, the symptom of that disease will eventually dry up. One day Jesus cursed a fig tree saying, 'From this day no man shall eat of thy fruit.' As far as He was concerned, the tree was cursed that very moment. But the leaves did not wither and fall until the next day. The roots had dried the day before, but it took time for the final result to reach the leaves. When Jesus Christ destroyed the curse of the law, He killed the roots of sickness.

"Sickness is the effect of sin, which is the curse of the law. The work of Christ destroyed the roots of illness. A person's faith enables the leaves of sickness to wither and fall away.

"The Bible tells us that when God brought the Israelites through the wilderness there was not a feeble person among all the tribes. There was an estimated two or three million people. Not one little baby had the cholic; not one old man had arthritic joints. No one had cancer. Over two and a half to three—million people, and not one person was sick. These people were under the dispensation of the law. They were not under the dispensation of grace and mercy. The Bible says, in the Book of Corinthians, that all of the things that happened to the Israelites were an example for us. But remember this: the word of God says, in the Book of Hebrews, that we now have a better priesthood. We have a better law, a better mercy and dispensation of grace. It's very logical to me that if God, under the dispensation of law and judgment, could bring three million people into a place of health and victory, why not Jesus Christ, who was a shadow of better things to come? Jesus Christ is that thing to come. He is the new priest and the Bible said that He is the High Priest that can be touched by the feelings of our infirmities.

"David, in the 103rd Psalm, through the inspiration of the Holy Spirit, shouted. 'Bless the Lord, oh my soul and all that's within me. Bless His Holy Name.' And he said, in the same breath, '. . . Who forgiveth all thy eniquities, who healeth all thy diseases.' David must have had great confidence that God would heal anyone that would believe Him and trust Him. That's the secret of divine healing. The word of God says, 'Faith cometh by hearing and hearing by the word of God.' What amazes me is that the opponents of divine healing only know three scriptures. They can relate to you Job's boils, Timothy's sore stomach, and Paul's thorn in the flesh. They have those down pat, but they can't give you one scripture that will build faith for physical healing.

"The Bible says 'Many are the afflictions of the righteous.' The word, 'affliction' in it's original translation means, temptation, trial, persecution or tribulation. It never refers to sickness. But if it did refer to sickness, you have to finish that verse in Psalms. It says, 'But the Lord delivereth them out of all of them.' Faith cometh by hearing and hearing by the word of God. Jesus said, 'By your traditions, you made the word of God of non-effect.' What He meant was, you've stripped it; you've made it powerless. Many people cop out on God's healing power. Instead of preaching a positive faith message that builds confidence in people's hearts, they preach an adverse message that strips people of their faith; destroys their confidence and gives them a spiritual complex.

"I've heard many say that sometimes we suffer for God's glory. We're going through the furnace of affliction because God sometimes has to bring us through these sicknesses and afflictions to make us better Christians. I refute that totally. I'll tell you why. I'm a father and I have three beautiful little daughters and occasionally I do have to spank my children. But do you think that I, as a loving father, would take a cancer germ and place that in my little girl's body? You know I wouldn't and neither would you. No dedicated parent would. You'd have to be a perverted parent to use sickness and suffering to correct your child.

"God is a better father than we are. The Bible says, 'If ye, being evil, know how to give good gifts to your children, how much more shall the Heavenly Father give good things to those that love Him.' It just doesn't make sense, on the one hand, to preach that God is a God of love and compassion and then, in the next breath, say that God has afflicted everybody and it is God's Will that we die with cancer or something worse."

CHAPTER XII

"Healing, Religion, and Psychology (or Is It the Other Way Around?)"

I want to pursue the phrase "all sickness is caused by sin" a bit further. I have not said all I want to say on the subject and neither has Vic. He is just as concerned that this is an oversimplification of his view as I am convinced that it has been the foundation for most faith healing ministries.

I am greatly concerned about the psychological factors surrounding a healing ministry—both at the front and the back; in terms of both cause and effect; motivation and backlash.

It has been said many times that it is more important to know what kind of fellow has a germ than what kind of germ has a fellow.

Once again, you are going to have to bear with me while we define certain terms and concepts which relate to the subject at hand. Psychology deals with repressed matter. Repressed matter is the result of ideas filtering from one's conscious mind through his subconscious mind, ultimately to his unconscious self. The unconscious self takes the repressed matter, screws it up real good, and then throws it back into the conscious mind in a totally different form, the result being chaotic. Let me show you how this works.

You commit an act of wrong. For hours after, it stays on your mind. You know you have committed an act of wrong against God and it preys on your mind. The next day you don't worry about it so much. In fact, you hardly think about it at all. This is because the deed is slowly slipping into your subconscious mind. Other than a general feeling of guilt, the specific act is gone from your mind. Soon you forget the matter completely as far as your conscious mind is concerned. But the deed is far from gone. It lives as a part of the permanent furniture of your unconscious mind.

Soon, the corpse begins to rise. It has lain on the bottom of an unconscious sea long enough. The lungs of guilt begin to fill. The sin rises once again to the conscious mind, but in a different form! The wrong rises, not in its original form—but as anger or frustration, or despair.

The person to whom this occurs does not know what has happened. He is a bundle of nerves. His entire personality becomes lopsided. The truth is that he has been a victim of the powerful complexity of his own mind.

Eighty percent of all hospital beds are filled with people whose emotions put them there. Seventy-five percent of all the people in mental institutions could go home tomorrow if they could be convinced they were forgiven.

All this means is what we have known for a long time: that many physical ills are rooted in mental trouble.

Conversely, this thinking reveals to us the powerful influence of the mind over the body. In January, 1957,

Fort Worth, Texas, a Mrs. Covington gave birth to a baby by means of Caesarean section. The operation involved post-hypnosis. She was told she would feel no pain during the operation. She was also told that there would be less bleeding during the operation. The surgeon said later that there was markedly less bleeding due to hypnosis than during a normal operation. She also needed no pain killing drug, simply because it had been suggested to her under hypnosis that she would feel no pain. This is an example of the tremendous power of the mind over the body.

If it appears I am rambling, forgive me, for I am not. Look with me for a moment at the place of suggestion in healing, primarily at the point of negative reaction.

Mrs. X. stands at the back of a healing line. She is sick: sick in mind; sick in body; sick in spirit. She has to be terribly ill or else she would not be standing where she is, parading her sickness in a public healing line.

What is Mrs. X. thinking as she stands there? I am afraid she is thinking she is ill because, among other reasons possibly, God is angry at her. Why? Because she has heard, at sometime, the proposition, "all sickness is caused by sin." She is sick. She has sinned. God must be angry. At least she is out of favor with Him.

Suddenly, Mrs. X. hears the voice of the faith healer thundering across the loud speaker. He is telling her that her illness is not ordained of God.

The evening passes quickly. Mrs. X. finds herself standing before the man of God. He suggests to her that her pain is gone, and, praise God, it is! "It's gone, it's gone, praise God! It's gone! God is no longer angry. My sin is forgiven. God and I are no longer estranged."

Several weeks pass by. The crusade is over. The man

of God has left town. Mrs. X. is at home, alone with her feelings. Tears are rolling down her cheeks. Her pain is back! What does this mean?

Mrs. X. has three alternatives: she can decide that the faith healer is a fraud. This alternative is completely out of the question. What right does she, Mrs. X., have to question the credibility of a man of God? Her second alternative is to think that God is not real. This she could never do. Her third alternative is to conclude that, for some reason, she does not fully comprehend, God has not found her worthy of forgiveness. She is driven, by this conclusion, to a state of mind far worse than before she went to the healer, for now it appears that she has no hope of even pleasing God, much less being well.

Mrs. X. is now in worse condition mentally than when she first went to church. Then, at least, she had hope. Now her attitude is marked with futility and hopelessness for, in her mind, God has found her unworthy to be healed. Her court of last appeal has found her guilty. Her pain is back! She is no longer healed. She was never healed. She was healed for a time, but no longer. Her pain is back! Where does she go from here? She has but two alternatives: she goes to a psychiatrist if she has the money. If not, she lets her new-found despair drive her to hopeless futility. An eminent psychologist of the sixties, A. Graham Ikin, stated that the upsurge in psychoanalysis was, in the sixties, directly related to the backlash of the disenchanted from faith healing crusades.

Let's put it this way: either Mrs. X. doesn't have the ability to have enough faith or, for some reason, God has decided that she is not worthy of being forgiven; thus driving Mrs. X. into a deeper repression and a deeper sense of guilt and abandonment than before she ever went to a healing service.

Vic: "First, let me say that any preacher who would preach that you are sick because you are sinful is totally off the beam. That is not what God's Word says! I do not preach this doctrine, which I think is totally misleading.

"My mode of preaching is this: I am like a doctor with a cure. I expose a person's need by the spirit, and by good sound, simple preaching. Then, I immediately offer a solution; not one that gives temporary relief and then drives to despair. I offer a new relationship in Jesus Christ.

"This is what brings people to Christ. If a person goes to a doctor, but doesn't know he has a particular disease, he is not too concerned. But if that person understands the nature of his condition, then he will want to be healed.

"I agree that there have been some persons, parading under the guise of God's men, who have made a mockery of God's plan for healing. Some of these men, frankly, should have been out building fences, because they are not knowledgeable in the field they represent. I have always heard that a little knowledge is a dangerous thing. This, to me, is like a horse doctor trying to transplant a kidney.

"There is one element that I stress constantly to people that I lead to Jesus Christ. It is called a *powerful positive confession*. Matthew 12:34 says that out of the heart the mouth speaketh. From the moment a person first believes, he lets his mouth, his voice become an expression of his faith or an expression of his doubt. When a person comes to Jesus Christ, according to Romans 10:9, he believes with his heart, but he confesses with his mouth.

"This means that no person can keep his salvation strong and vital unless he is willing constantly to keep on confessing that Jesus Christ is his Lord and Saviour.

"We are not saved by our feeling, but by our faith. Unfortunately, many times a Christian has the temptation to doubt that he is a Christian. Almost every Christian, at some point, goes through a period of doubt. The devil, and circumstances in general, make a person doubt that he ever was a Christian in the first place, or that his sins were ever forgiven.

"What is the only thing that can overcome this kind of problem in a Christian's life? He has to reaffirm, or step up the process of confessing his faith. A person must, by faith, confess his faith even when he may not *feel* he is saved. If he doesn't do this, he will simply slide deeper into doubt. If he does keep confessing, he will ultimately strengthen his faith. We believe in Jesus Christ, whom we have not seen. It is our job to build up that belief by confession—constantly!

"This same process of continual confession also works with regard to physical healing. It's like the fig tree we discussed earlier. When a person is prayed for, the roots of the illness, or the cause of the symptom, dies. But the symptom, like the green leaves on the fig tree, lingers. I've seen people prayed for regarding, for instance, cancer. Doctors are constantly trying to find something that will kill the cancer cells, but not at the same time kill all the other good cells. Cobalt and radium treatments are the closest things they have found. So they have proven that cancer has a life to it. Now you can kill the life—the malignant tumor—but the cancer may linger as far as the symptom is concerned. Therefore, it doesn't look like it's gone just because all symptoms do not vanish overnight. But the life of the cancer is dead.

"This is where confession must play a big part. When a person comes to Jesus Christ, the color of his hair doesn't change. His fingernails don't grow any faster. His body weight doesn't increase ten pounds over night. Basically, he's the same human being. His character, his personality—almost everything about him—stays the same. But one thing is different: *the person knows that a spiritual change has taken place in his heart.* At this point, confession becomes extremely vital. When people are prayed for regarding healing, they must learn to confess the confession of faith.

"Let me apply this to the person whose pain leaves, and then returns a couple of days later. The person concludes he hasn't been healed. I always say to this person, 'You have nullified—destroyed—the very thing that God did in your body the first time by faith. You should be saying, 'This returning symptom of pain is a lie because God has healed me!' Instead of confessing what God says in His Word, the person is confessing his own weak feelings about the symptom.

"This is like the devil coming to a person and saying, 'You looked lustfully at that woman: you have already thought about it; you may as well go ahead and commit the act.' If one allows it, this type thinking will grow until the person will go ahead and sin. One must be able to cast this type thought from his mind by saying, 'I am saved by the blood of Christ. This is an accomplished fact. I accept it. And I will be true to it.' The Bible says resist the devil and he will flee from you. The same is true when Satan tries to tell you that you have not been healed. Anything that God gives you, the devil is going to try to take away. How many new converts have backslidden because, instead of accepting what God said in His Word about their conversion, they listened to the doubts of the devil and started confessing that they weren't saved. The same element of confession is vital in keeping your faith and confession alive regarding healing.

CHAPTER XIII

"First Salvation—Then Healing (or Is It the Other Way Around?)"

Since I have used the phrase "or is it the other way around?" in two chapter headings, perhaps I should give an explanation for its usage. Ernie Kovaks was a T.V. comic from my youth. He was, in fact, one of the first T.V. comedians. (I was very young.) He used to do a skit where he would answer fictitious questions that fictitious callers would send in.

One of the callers asked him to give the name of the animal with the head of a human and the body of a horse, and also the name of the animal with the head of a horse and the body of a human.

He would quickly identify each of the two by name, giving intricate details about both animals. Then he would pause and say, "or is it the other way around?"

Through the years the story has stayed with me. One reason it has lingered is that I am continually running into dual situations when I cannot be certain but that it is really the other way around. Let me show you how this works: Mahayana is the name for Northern Buddhism, while Hinayana is the name for Southern Buddhism—or is it the other way round? Hawaii is the forty-ninth state and Alaska is the fiftieth—or is it the other way around?

Lest I put you to sleep with this analogy, let me apply it to the subject at hand. Imagine with me a faith healer conducting a television question-answer program in the style of Ernie Kovacs. Someone sends in the following question: Which is more important, spiritual salvation or physical healing?"

I have a feeling—really it is more than a feeling; more like a conviction, that the faith healer's answer, if he were as honest as Ernie Kovacs, would be something like this: "The answer to the question as to which is more important, spiritual salvation or physical healing is very simple: spiritual salvation is quite definitely the most important and primary while physical healing, although important, is certainly secondary . . . or is it the other way around?"

If this appears too subtle, let me come more directly to the point. When I attend the service of many faith healers, I get one or all of the following impressions: 1.) that salvation and healing are at least synonymous 2.) that a saved person should be well and a well person should be saved 3.) that, at most, physical healing is the central doctrine of Christianity.

Perhaps I should be more explicit about my use of the word, central. The 19th century was one that witnessed the birth of four sects: Jehovah's Witness (1872), Seventh Day Adventists (1844), Mormonism (1830), and Christian Science (1899).

Each of these four sects grew out of a deficiency in the churches of the nineteenth century. Each sect, in an effort to reaffirm an essential facet of the gospel of Christ, went too far and moved a secondary doctrine to the center in terms of the emphasis it was given. Brother Russell was concerned over a lack of attention to the second coming of Christ. Thus Jehovah's Witness was born.

Mrs. White became concerned over the lack of respect that was given to the Sabbath. Out of this grew Seventh Day Adventists.

Joseph Smith decided that marriage for the dead and baptism for the dead deserved more attention. Thus came Mormonism. Finally, Mary Baker Glover Patterson Eddy was appalled at the lack of attention that was given in Christian circles to divine, or physical, bodily healing. Out of this grew Christian Science.

Each sect began with good intentions. Each group was pointing up a lack in nineteenth century commitment to Jesus Christ. Each group produced a book to serve as an appendix to the Bible. Each group went too far in that the central doctrine of redemption through Jesus Christ was moved to a secondary position and a secondary doctrine—either a day, or the second coming of Christ, or physical healing—was given the central position.

I do not want to be guilty of oversimplifying any terms which we are using, or of misstating another person's position. Permit me to take time to clarify some of the meanings which I find in various doctrinal concepts. In the context of a discussion about divine healing, the terms "pain" and suffering" are usually lumped in with the word "sickness" and all of these are considered to be bad; or at least outside the realm of the will of God for a human being.

It should be noted that the word "pain" has a very limited and fairly shallow meaning when thrown in with the word "suffering" which can have a much deeper meaning; and, I sincerely believe, a much loftier meaning.

Much has been written about animal pain. The conclusion has been that animals know very little about pain as humans know it. We do not know all the reasons for this. One reason appears to be that animals do not have the capability to understand all the consequences that can arise from their actions. To the extent that they do instinctively become aware of potential threat, pain appears to surface more strongly. Let me try to illustrate some of the degrees of pain that can be experienced as we move from a purely animal basis to the human plain.

Once I watched three crabs on the seashore. One of the crabs was eating the other, while a third was apparently enjoying lunch on the second. It was difficult to locate pain in all of this.

On another occasion I watched a bird nest burning. The nest contained several baby birds. They were making noises which obviously denoted some degree of pain. However, there was a mother bird circling the outside of the nest, trying to get through the flames. She was screeching in a way that made me feel that, although she was not burning, the suffering of the mother bird was superior to what was happening to the birds being burned with the nest. Somehow, there was, in that experience, a faint glimpse of the difference between pain on the one hand and suffering on the other; although the degree of difference was in no way measurable.

Let me move to an Old Testament prophet, Hosea. This man dearly loved his wife Gomer. His wife left him and their children and went away with other men. Hosea would cry out in the night for Gomer. His suffering was almost greater than he could bear. Because he knew more than a bird about life, I would have to say that, just as the mother bird's suffering was greater than the baby birds', Hosea's suffering was greater than the mother bird's.

The Bible tells us that God had a reason for allowing Hosea to suffer. He was using the prophet's pain as a telescope to show him, by his wife going away, how God suffered when His people go away from Him.

Through this experience of suffering and pain, God was trying to make a better prophet out of Hosea. Hosea's suffering was greater than the mother bird, and God's suffering was greater than Hosea's. God apparently used experiences of suffering with His prophets to try to teach them how God suffered. There was value in all this for God's ultimate aim, both for His prophets and His people, was redemptive—which is the central theme of the Bible. God was not always interested in merely pleasing people, but in saving them.

God, through men like Hosea, was preparing the world for the coming of Jesus Christ who would suffer and die, that all people might be saved.

It is too easy, or simple, to say that Christ suffered so that no one else would have to suffer. Paul, the apostle, suffered. And I am not merely speaking of his thorn in the flesh, which may have been anything from poor eyesight to some form of personal temptation. Paul said he died daily. At another point he said that, in coming to Christ, he suffered the loss of all things. At another point he said he gloried in his sufferings because they made him a part of the sufferings of Jesus Christ. Again he said that his sufferings were not worthy to be compared to the sufferings of Christ.

In the eighth chapter of Romans, Paul said, "Who shall separate us from the love of Christ? shall tribulation, or distress, or persecution, or famine, or nakedness, or peril or sword? (v. 35)." Then he added a most significant word: "Nay in all these things, we are more than conquerors through Him that loved us (v. 37)." God did not save men *from* these things so much as he saved them *in* these adversities. Even God's people—witness the early Christian martyrs—will sometimes receive great hammer blows of suffering. This happens to saints and sinners alike. The rain falls on both the just and the unjust. But the same hammer that breaks the glass, forges the steel. The same experience that makes one person bitter can make another better.

I am not trying to create an excuse for failure, either on God's part or man's. I am rather trying to steer away from easy answers to difficult problems that befall man—problems that may not be quite as perplexing if they can be viewed from the centrality of God's redemptive process for man which extends throughout all eternity.

Helmut Thielecke, a noted German theologian, once remarked that one of the principle deficiencies of Western theology was that we were hopeless problem solvers. For Western man, every problem had to have a solution. We have, in Thielecke's view, no capacity for bearing up under a burden that must be borne; for living with a problem. Living in Germany during the war years, Thielecke knew what it meant to watch people bear up under a burden that would not go away. It is easy, he went on to suggest, for preachers to present problem solving theology in a nation that has won all it's wars, has plenty to eat, and is literally the richest and most powerful nation in the world. His conclusion was that there is a place in the redemptive theology of Jesus Christ for the bearing of burdens, the enduring of suffering and pain, in the name of Jesus Christ, and for His glory.

When I was in the seminary, a minister spoke one day in chapel on the subject: "Faith, Even When the Ship Sinks." He used the passage of scripture where Jesus was out on the sea one night with His disciples and a storm arose. Jesus was asleep in the boat. The disciples cried, "Master, save us! We perish!" Jesus awoke and stilled the storm. Then He turned to His disciples and asked, "Where is your faith?" The speaker made the point that Jesus was not saying, "didn't you know I would save you?" He was rather asking, "do you only have faith in Me so long as the ship doesn't sink?"

The speaker, Dr. Warren Hultgren, of Tulsa, Oklahoma, then recounted a story that had been printed in Reader's Digest. It was the story of two separate events that had occurred several years apart during the same decade. The first involved a ship that encountered a severe storm as it passed around a cape in the South Seas. The storm was worse than any of the saliors had ever seen. They were caught up in fear. They began to fall on their knees and to pray that God would save them. The ship broke as it washed up on a sand bar. Of the over two hundred sailors on the ship, none died. They all made it to shore safely. As a result, many of the sailors, like Jonah, became preachers. They went across the land telling others what God had done.

Several years later, another ship was caught in a storm while passing the same cape .The storm was more severe than any of the sailors had ever seen. Like the sailors years before, they fell on their knees and prayed that God would spare them. The ship sank, and all the sailors died.

The Readers Digest story asked this question: Was it a matter that the sailors in the first experience prayed harder, or better; or is there such a thing as having faith, even when the ship sinks?

There is room, in my opinion, for all that I am saying and also a valid approach to divine healing, so long as one does not lose sight of the centrality of the redemptive process of Jesus Christ who came *primarily* "to seek and to save that which is lost."

I will agree with any person or group on this earth that suffering and sickness are foul things. Some have said that suffering makes saints. This statement is untrue. Suffering is more likely to make rebellious cynics or querulous neurotics. The saints have not been made saints because of suffering, but in spite of it. It has been their reaction to suffering that made saintliness, not the suffering itself.

I am saying, in summary, that suffering must be seen as more than just physical or mental disorder. It must be seen also as emotional and spiritual rupture, both within and without a personality. Which is worse, a broken bone, or a betrayed, lonely deafeated, broken heart? Who suffers more? One who stutters, or walks with a limp, or one who sobs the night through with a heart torn to shreds by betrayal or disgrace?

In studying the New Testament, it appears to me that Jesus sought for a restoring of harmony to a whole personality and not just the straightening of a limb.

I do not fault a sincere man of God for holding out to a sick and suffering human being what may be his last ray of hope and relief before he leaves this earth. I rather cast my vote for the primacy of redemption and ask the question, has anything good ever come out of suffering other than the purchase of our salvation by Jesus Christ?

Empirically speaking, I must add that, while pastoring two churches, I surely witnessed a number of persons who spent their last days on this earth glorifying

God, even in spite of their suffering.

Vic: "C. A., let me inject, at this point, my opinion that, quite honestly, everything you have just said has a negative ring to it. Forgive me for being so blunt, but your words are quite typical of many people who look for excuses for failure; who think they must apologize for God.

"Most ministers I know who try to find value in pain aren't trying to do very much about relieving pain. You can ask me if I know of any people who apparently live good decent lives, who are not Christians, and I'll say yes. But does this mean that these people do not need to be saved? Or that we should stop preaching salvation and simply help everyone to be good?

"So you know of people who didn't let their pain make them bitter? Does that mean they are better off with the pain, or without it? Does that mean we should simply help people not to be bitter in their pain? Or should we help them find the one who has promised to take the pain away?

I refuse to spend my time explaining pain and apologizing for God. I'm going to spend my time preaching the saving power of Christ to a lost world, and the healing power of Christ to a sick world.

C. A.: "Vic, I hear you saying that salvation and healing are synonomous in a sense, to the extent that a person can neither be saved without human instrumentality, nor can he be healed without human instrumentality. Does this mean that a person cannot be sure he has been saved until he has been healed? And if he is healed, then if or when the sickness returns, does this mean that the person has lost his salvation? How do you separate these two?"

Vic: "When Jesus ministered on this earth, some-

times the people He healed knew nothing about salvation. A man was blind and Jesus healed him. The
Pharisees went to the man and said, 'tell us about this
person who healed you.' The man replied, 'I don't
know anything about Him. I only know I was blind
and now I see.' Later, Jesus found the man and asked
him if he believed in the Son of God. The man asked,
who is the Son of God that I might believe on Him?'
Jesus said, 'I am the Son of God.' This showed Jesus'
healing ministry without a salvation ministry.

"On another occasion, four men lowered their friend
down through the roof of a house were Jesus was teaching. The man was afflicted with the palsy. He was unable to walk. Jesus said to him, 'Thy sins be forgiven.'
Some of the critics of Jesus in the group said, 'who is
this that speaks blasphemy? Who can forgive but God
alone?'

"Jesus said, 'which is easier for me to say, 'thy sins
be forgiven, or rise, take up thy bed and walk? But I
have done this that you may know that the Son of God
has power to forgive sin on earth.'

"Jesus always combined spiritual healing with physical healing. He reached the very souls of men by touch-
ing their outer needs. Mahatma Ghandi once said that
even God would not be foolish enough to appear to
a starving man in any other form than a loaf of bread.
It is foolish to appear to a person who is starving and
preach a message of God's abundant life until you
feed that person.

"It is foolish to come to a dying, suffering person
and talk of the God of the by and by, with all His love
and mercy, power and love, who doesn't have enough
power and compassion to meet that person's needs now!

"People who come to my crusades don't have an

understanding of all this theology of divine healing. They simply come to my services because they have a need to be healed. And I don't feel like I have a right only to preach to them that part of the Bible they *didn't* come for and hide from them that portion that they *did* come for.

"Peter preached both sides of the atonement in I Peter 2:24. First, he said, '. . . Himself took our sins in His own body upon the tree that we, being dead to sin, might live unto righteousness.' Then he went on to say in the same verse, '. . . by whose stripes ye were healed.'

"It is perfectly logical to me that if one never preached the message of salvation, then no one would ever be saved, for 'faith comes by hearing and hearing by the word of God.'

"It is also logical to me that unless a preacher preaches that portion of God's Word which builds positive faith for physical healing, then healing will not come.

"Let me give a little background. Before dealing with salvation and healing, we must remember that sin and sickness are synonomous and yet they are not synonomous.

"Sin and sickness came about because of the Fall, when Adam and Eve committed high treason against God. They had been made in the image and likeness of God. They had been made to live forever in the Garden of Eden. God told them, the day they sinned, they would die. He meant both spiritually and physically they would die. Spiritual death began to operate in their lives immediately after their sin, for they were driven from the Garden. This is what spiritual death means—separation and alienation from God.

"Physical death also began to operate in their lives immediately because of their sin, their high treason against God. Adam and Eve died, we all know that. We also know that every human being from Adam and Eve died except Enoch and Elijah. The Bible says that in Adam all die but in Christ, the second Adam, all are made alive.

"Physical death, disease and affliction came about because of the Fall. The Bible says Jesus Christ came to restore all things. He came to restore us to a position before God, not only where we can walk in righteousness and in fellowship with God, but also where we can be restored to health. That's what Peter said: '. . . (Jesus) took our sins in His own body on the tree that we might live unto righteousness.' He also said, '. . . by whose stripes ye were healed.' Wouldn't it be foolish to say that Jesus suffered those thirty-nine stripes on his back (by the way, there are thirty-nine categories of sickness) and we turn around and reject what it can mean to us?

"Some people reject preaching about the blood of Jesus Christ. Others reject the resurrection, or the deity of Christ. "Those people who reject these doctrines cannot be saved. Similarly, those who reject the Lord's broken body cannot be healed. In 1st Corinthians, Paul writes about communion. For years traditionalists have used the scripture where Paul said, 'if one eats and drinks Christ's Body unworthily, he is eating himself damnation because he does not rightly discern the Lord's Body.' Paul concluded by adding, 'there are so many weak and sickly among you.'

"Jesus was an exact type of the Levitical Lamb. When the Levitical Lamb was slain, the blood was sprinkled on the doorpost. This kept the death angel from coming and taking it's toll upon God's people. Then God commanded the people to eat the flesh of the Passover Lamb. When they did this, the flesh literally became 'bone of their bone, flesh of their flesh, blood of their blood.' Then God said, 'I am Jehovah Refah, or I am the Lord that healeth thee (Exodus 15:26).

"One of God's seven redemptive names was 'I am the Lord that healeth thee.' This meant that God was going to be the people's Great Physician through the Passover Lamb and their faith in Him. The Psalms tell us that when God brought the people out of the wilderness, there was not one feeble person among all the tribes. Why was this? It was because the people not only accepted the blood for salvation from the death angel, they also accepted the Passover Lamb, thus making God their Great Physician. They trusted in the Physician. In fact, at one point in the Old Testament, we find that God cursed certain people who trusted in medicine and herbs in Egypt instead of God's Hand and God's mighty power.

C.A.: "I get what you are saying: that it is both salvation and healing—not either salvation or healing. But which one is first? Do you feel that salvation—redemption—getting saved is the central facet of the gospel or do you feel that divine healing, getting your body well, is the central facet of the gospel?"

Vic: "I believe that salvation is imperative. I think anyone with spiritual common sense would rather see a man go to heaven sick than a man go to hell well. That, to me, is very good common sense. However, my feeling is that Jesus Christ died to pay the price and penalty for both the body and the soul. There is therefore no reason why we should not preach the full gospel for body, mind, and soul. In III John 2, the Bible says, 'Beloved, I wish above all things that thou mayest prosper and be in health even as thy soul prosper.' That verse places as much stress on physical health as it does spiritual health."

C. A.: "In using the word 'central', what I am asking is which of the two do you consider more important—salvation or healing? You used the word 'imperative' regarding salvation. Can one extrapolate from this that you also consider it more important than anything else in the gospel?

"I have heard you say in your crusades that the greatest miracle is salvation, and that's why you call people to be saved in every service. However, I am concerned that in actual practice, the opposite appears to be true—that healing is not only on an equal level with salvation, but has become more important. It is simple to say that these both—salvation and healing—go together. But is it valid to make healing the central, or predominant emphasis of the gospel to the extent that it gets more emphasis than even salvation?"

Vic: "When you study Jesus' ministry, you find that 75 percent of His ministry was healing the sick and casting out demons. When you study the apostles, ministries in the Book of Acts, you find the early church was not really kicked off in great grandstand glory on the day of Pentecost. It was a short time later when Peter raised a man who was lame at the Temple gate and thousands came wondering what was happening. Through that miracle, Peter preached to thousands of people saying, 'Why look ye so earnestly upon us as through our own power of holiness we made this man whole?' He said, 'We've done it in the name of Jesus Christ of Nazareth whom you crucified.' Then he took that opportunity to preach the message about Jesus Christ, who He was and why He came to die.

"The Bible says 5,000 were added to the church because of that miracle.

"When Paul was shipwrecked on the island of Malta, we find that he had a great testimony among the people there because he healed the chief's father-in-law. He healed many others that came to him.

"Jesus' ministry was a healing ministry. He was either healing, had just come from healing or was on his way to heal. Why was this? First, Jesus knew that healing would attract people in grandstand glory. Second, He loved people. He was against sickness. He wanted to rub the balm of Giliad into their suffering and afflicted bodies. 'We are the salt of the earth.' He said, 'and we are to be ground into the decaying carcasses of this unregenerate society.'

"Yes, I emphasize physical healing. Yet, it has never eclipsed the emphasis of my ministry on spiritual salvation. The statistics prove that. Although I emphasize physical healing, praying for thousands of people, this ministry still is winning a greater percentage of people to Jesus Christ than all of those who oppose this type ministry.

"I feel it is not only a valid ministry, but also a balanced ministry because I don't preach merely on divine healing. I preach Jesus Christ. I incorporate into Christ His saving power, His healing power, and His strengthening power. I talk about Christian growth. I talk about the coming of Jesus Christ. I talk about witnessing. I happen to believe that, as far as deliverance ministries go, this is the most balanced ministry in our generation. I believe God has made it so. I believe that's the reason people respond to it.

"I have followed some healing ministries and watched them go down hill because they over-emphasized the message of divine healing. In fact, I refute and disdain the very terminology of the faith healer because I am not a healer. I am an evangelistic servant of Christ who preaches the full council of God. In Mark 16, Jesus said to His followers, 'Go ye into all the world and preach the gospel to every creature and he that believeth and is baptised is saved and he that believeth not is damned.' But He didn't stop there. Jesus went on to say, 'And these signs shall follow them that believe and in my name they shall cast out demons; they shall speak with new tongues; they shall take up serpents. If they drank any deadly thing, it shall not hurt them.' Then He went on to say, 'They shall lay hands on the sick and they shall recover.' The Bible says that they went everywhere preaching the word, the Lord working with them and confirming the word with signs following.

"Philip would have never converted the heathen city of Samaria if he had been nothing but a preacher. The Bible says, 'They gave heed onto the things that Philip spake because they saw the miracle he did.' If you trace the Book of Acts, you find that only where miracles accompanied the ministry of God's servants, did the heathen readily and easily listen to the gospel. I went to Durango, Mexico, about a year and a half ago for a crusade. Durango is a city of over 200,000 people. In 580 years of history, that city has never had over six or seven–hundred believers in Christ. The pastors said they had struggled for years to get people saved and had only a few converted. I had over seven-thousand come to Jesus Christ in two nights and they readily and wonderously accepted the Lord when they saw the word of God confirmed with signs following.

"Physical healing in a ministry like mine is very important. I believe it is an attractive thing. Many people come to my crusades with no intent of accepting Jesus Christ. They come to be healed. But the beautiful thing about it is that, once God heals your body, once you experience a physical miracle, it is hard to reject and neglect the God that did such a wonderful thing for your life."

CHAPTER XIV

"Tell No Man"

"God Can Do Anything But Fail." That was the title of a song we used to sing when I was growing up. This title meets all the requirements of good logic so far as I am concerned. The very word 'God' denotes, to one's mind, the concept of a being who has all power, wisdom and nobility. Therefore, logic would follow this pattern: 1.) Either God is or God is not. 2.) If God is not, He can do nothing— (for He is not). 3.) If God is, then He can do anything— (simply because He is).

I could never understand a person so illogical that he was willing to believe in God, but made this Being into one more like man than God. As I stated in the outset of this book, the only big hurdle I find in an idea of God is accepting the basic premise that there is a God. Beyond that, or having decided to accept this premise, why would one want or even think it possible to place limitations on God? The writer of Hebrews says, 'He that cometh to God must believe that He is." This may sound like an incomplete sentence. But what else need be said of God's essence—His nature—than that He is?

Therefore, what we are exploring in these pages is not God's *power,* but His *plan.* We are not raising questions about what God can or cannot do, but how

He has chosen to deal with people—reveal His nature and plan for people.

How does this relate to divine healing? Simply in this way: we are not pursuing whether, granting there is a God, He can and does heal people. We are rather pursuing how He goes about it in general, and the use He makes of human instruments in particular: namely, faith healers.

Will Rogers has been credited with saying he never met a man he didn't like. I never met a faith healer I did like until I met Vic Coburn. I admire his consistency theologically. I do not mean here that Vic's thinking is consistent with what I think is correct theologically, for that is of no importance. Rather, I find him consistent in practice with his own theological views—in that he places fewer conditions of God's power than any man I have seen in the realm of divine healing practice. In short, he does not protect himself from failure. More than any other faith healer (although Vic rejects the phrase) he subscribes, both in theory and in practice, to the premise that God can do anything but fail. This, to me, is how it ought to be with a minister. Surely, if there is a God, He can do anything.

There is still, however, a matter here that does concern me—and that is the public use of God's power for personal gain.

At a certain point in my life, I was affected, possibly more than any single book I've ever read, by a book written by a woman, Adella Rogers St. John, entitled, *Tell No Man*. It is the story of a successful young businessman, who quit his job and became a minister for one reason: he wanted to try to discover if the power of God to work in human lives—the same power evidenced in the ministry of Jesus Christ as He went about helping people—was still available today. He decided that, if it was available, it would come to a man who gave himself in complete and selfless dedication to the teachings and principles of Jesus Christ.

The young minister faced several immediate tests. First, he had an extremely wealthy grandmother who had written into her will that her only grandson would inherit all her fortune, only if he were not a minister. Second, he had a wife who was accustomed to the life as a wife of a $50,000 a year business executive, and who did not even believe in God, much less the new calling of her husband.

The young man was faced with a paradoxical dilemma. On the one hand, he desperately wanted to witness to his wife regarding the power of God that was available to heal broken hearts and broken bodies. On the other hand, he was deeply impressed with the style of Jesus that was, to him, twofold: first, Jesus helped and/or healed everyone who came to Him; second, He had a way of drawing attention to the healing power of God, but not necessarily to the Healer; namely Himself. In fact, on several occasions, Jesus instructed the person he healed to go and "tell no man of the one who did these works."

Two things happened to the minister. First, he found that he had the insight, not only to heal, but also to look into the mind and heart of people and discern their need. Second, his wife left him, because he refused to use the power God was giving him to do what Jesus refused to do: make of it a publicity tool for his own advantage.

In the conclusion, God surprises the young man. He had all but lost hope. He had been able to help everyone but himself, and his wife, whom he dearly loved

and prayed for daily. In the closing scene, his wife
brings to him a young person who, the wife knows for
certain, has just died in a knifing accident. The minister falls down beside the young person and commands
God that He put life in the limp body before him.

In that climactic scene, the wife receives from God
the sign she had asked for, but the husband had not
compromised his commitment in order for her to receive it.

I have never found it my place to question that
some men have a gift from God to extend a healing
touch to people in need. I have questioned why these
men did not have the courage, or faith, or guts, to
trust God to be their publicity agent, and to adopt the
practice to heal and to help, but to "tell no man of the
one who did these works." I passed this question to
Vic in the following way:

"I hear you using Jesus as an example that He did
a lot of healing. I do not concede as readily that He
publicized it quite as much as you might have inferred.
In fact, we have on record from some of His closest
followers that sometimes He did just the opposite.
Sometimes He told those whom He healed to go and
'tell no man of the one who did these works.'

"It appears to be a bit incongruous to be taking your
example from Jesus Christ who did heal a lot of people,
but didn't use it as a publicity vehicle; then to see a
faith healer go on national television and use his healings as his drawing card."

Vic: "Yes, but you have to realize one thing. Jesus
Christ was not yet revealed to the world as the Son of
God. Not one time did He publicly preach that He was
the Messiah until He died. Why did the apostles—
once they began their tremendous ministry in the Book

of Acts, when they were filled with the Holy Spirit and the church became a born church, inaugurated by the spirit of God—use healing as a calling card? The Bible says, "the great multitudes came together, they magnified the Lord, great and small. They went from house and door to door testifying to the power of Jesus Christ; what He could do, how He could save, how He could heal."

"Let's be rational. If you, for instance, were a medical scientist and suddenly you found a cure for cerebral palsy or for polio, or for cancer, would you think it humane to hide that cure and not tell the world about it because you found it and were afraid that you would exalt yourself? Would you be afraid people would say, 'Well look, he's just bragging because he found the cure for polio?' No. You would channel that cure into every medical outlet throughout the world because that cure worked. It's fool proof. Jesus Christ said, in John 14:12, 'He that believeth on me, the works that I do, shall he do also and greater works than these shall he do because I go on to my Father.'

"He also said, in Acts 1:11, 'But ye shall receive power after that the Holy Spirit has come on you and ye shall be witnesses both in Jerusalem, Judea, Samaria and the uttermost parts of the earth.' Jesus, Himself, said, after the Holy Spirit has come upon you, you will go throughout the world publicizing My power, publicizing the reality of My gospel.'

We publicize murders and rapes and robberies. Jesus Christ could not proclaim Himself to be the Messiah because the revelation of who Jesus really was did not come until after His ressurection. The disciples didn't even believe Jesus Christ was going to rise again. So that proves to me that they didn't really believe He was the Messiah. They didn't belive that He was the Christ. Many of them thought He was. But after He died, they lost that confidence. It was only after the ressurection of Jesus Christ that the great publicity of the gospel begin to spread its flaming influence all over the world. Yes, when a miracle happens, it needs to be publicized. Men publicize everything else. Men publicize the things that degrade the gospel. Madelyn Murray O'Hare can go on national television and can rip-off God's people. She can ban prayer and Bible reading in the schools. So I think every mighty work of God should be magnified and amplified. Don't we glorify God when we save someone? Billy Graham has sports stars and movie stars on his telecast. So does Kathryn Kuhlman and Oral Roberts. Why? Because they're trying to get credibility; trying to publicize to the world that a movie star who used to be a dope head and a pervert is now serving Jesus Christ. The same thing is true with healing. If we have to relate to what you've just asked me regarding healing, we have to relate to it regarding salvation. It would be wrong then to tell anybody that we won someone to Jesus Christ."

CHAPTER XV

"Scientifically Speaking"

In America there are two keys that will unlock almost any door: science and athletics. If you are either a scientist or an athlete, you are welcome almost any time, anywhere. In America we have these two, science and athletics; but the greatest of these is science.

If a problem is being approached "scientifically," it is being approached correctly—obviously. If a project is called a "scientific study," no one will question it. Introduce a man as a "scientist," and he will immediately gain an almost reverent respect from those around him. The word "science" is magic. It means honor. It carries a ring of nobility. If a statement is "scientific," it is probably true. Why? I don't know, except that we are dealing with the elite, highest circle of the New American Royalty, the medical profession.

The term "faith healing" evokes about as many negative vibrations as the term "science" does positive. When one hears "faith healer," or "faith healing," he is immediately either suspicious, afraid, bored, disgusted, or downright mad. The term "faith healing" automatically closes both as many doors and minds as the term "science" opens.

Yet, it was medical science that gave us blood-letting, to choose only one of many blunders along the way. The faith healer would have approached that feverish body and in the name of Jesus Christ, prayed for deliverance, leaving the men of science standing in the corner turning up their scientific noses at this unscientific approach. But have no fear, for here comes the doctor, in the name of medical science. What is he doing? He is drawing a pint—no—wait—a quart of blood from the feverish body. Ah, praise be to science!

The feverish body goes limp. The fever fades away, for the person is dead. "See there, the prayers of the faith healer didn't do any good. He gave us false hope. He kept us from taking Uncle Charlie to the hospital. Down with all the misguiding, misleading faith healers of the world . . . oh, and thank you, doctor, for coming. You did all you could. Uncle Charlie would have wanted us to give you this extra hundred. We will send along our Insurance number to your Middle Ages Answering Service tomorrow."

It took us decades to get medical science to admit what killed Uncle Charlie. When we finally did get the signed confession that taking all that blood did Charlie in, we passed up manslaughter and filed the case away under "scientific progress."

What I am trying to get at here is a little relativity —a little perspective. I have not only never written a book like this, I have never read one like it. And the openness and straightforwardness of Vic Coburn in the face of some pretty tough questioning makes the difference. That's why I want to be certain that I am at least as fair to Vic in this chapter as he frankly deserves.

I could have gone back into my files and pulled out a sizeable number of suits that have been brought against faith healers in the past—suits that related to a person charging the healer with injuring health, or retarding it, rather than aiding it.

I chose not to do this for it would not only be unfair

to Vic—who has never had a suit brought against him in nine years of breaking crutches and the like—but also to other men in the faith healing practice, who will never be able to match the pile of malpractice suits that our beloved medical profession has stacked up through the years.

I would like to meet the doctor who has been practicing (doesn't that word "practice" scare you a little?) medicine for nine years and has not had a malpractice suit brought against him. I don't question his existence. I simply have never met him. Probably Vic Coburn, in the past nine years, has prayed for more people than any single doctor in the country has been able to treat personally. To this day—not one 'malprayer' suit has been brought against Vic.

For those who are not against playing a game of "would you believe" every now and then, I think I may have run across a place where the paths of medical science and faith healing are crossing, in none other than the city where I not only grew up, but spent my seminary days, Fort Worth, Texas. I will leave the medicine men unidentified so they may proceed with their research and testing in their own way. It should also be noted that I have neither met these men personally, nor visited their clinic. My information comes to me from a close friend who was enrolled with the leaders of this investigative team in a seminar on mind control.

In substance, these men are convinced they have found a cure for cancer. To date, they have not recorded the number of test cases that should be required to meet the standards of an acceptable investigation. However, at this writing, they have had an astonishingly high success factor—between 80 percent to 90 percent. This is even more incredible when it is realized they have been dealing only with cases that have been diagnosed as terminal.

Their basic hypothesis is that cancer begins when the brain stops sending energy to certain cells. For cells to live, they must not only receive blood and oxygen, but also a direct supply of energy from the brain. As I understand it, they have a machine that is used to probe the ear lobe to pick up response—or lack of response—that would indicate that a nerve is falling down on the job of brain-to-tissue relay.

Then, as one would recharge a battery, they use a machine that recharges the sluggish nerve. Soon energy is once again flowing to the area, arresting the cancerous growth.

Let me move to a part of their procedure with a patient that especially intrigues me. Initially, before any testing takes place, the patient is interviewed. Listen to this: these doctors indicate that in almost all of the cases they have handled to this point, the individual will have had an extremely traumatic experience in the recent past—in most instances, beween six and nine months. There would have been the death of a loved one, or a divorce, or trouble with children. It appears, at least to these doctors, that there is some sort of direct relationship between the traumatic past experience, the short supply of energy flow from the brain to parts of the body, and, ultimately, the growth of cancer in the death of the related cells.

Listen to their next step, after initially interviewing the patient: (you will think you are under the evangelist's tent) they give the person suggestions in the most affirmative and strongest manner—that he or she is going to get well. They are convinced that, since the cancerous growth had an emotional base in the first place, the process will not be arrested unless the emotional factor is dealt with constructively and positively.

Now, for the clincher: the doctors say that one treatment—seeing the patient only one time—is sufficient for arresting the cancer *unless,* get this, the individual has not been made to believe that he or she is going to get well!

If that didn't ring some medical bells in the halls of the American Medical Association, this next tidbit will. My friend, who was in the Mind Control Seminar with one of the doctors, asked him what he thought of faith healers. In essence, this was his reply: "They've got the answer, I don't understand all they do and why, but they've got the answer."

I related to Vic the study these doctors were making and asked what relationship there might be between what they are doing and what he is doing.

Vic: "What they are doing is natural. What the anointed servant of God is doing is supernatural when he prays for the sick. The doctors rely upon natural energy to restimulate the cells of the brain to redirect energy to the portion of the body that is afflicted with cancer. I lay my hand upon a person, the energy comes from God through the power of the Holy Spirit that brings forth healing virtue. You remember when Jesus' garment was touched by the woman? The Bible says that as the woman who had the issue of blood touched the hem of Jesus' garment, virtue, or power, flowed from Him into her and she was cured of that disease.

"This is exactly what happens when I pray for someone or lay my hands on someone. The power of God flows through me to them.

"I'd like to relate a story pertaining to this, that's

exciting. Doctor John R. Lake, during the twenties and thirties, was a very successful healing evangelist in the country. He had a healing clinic in Spokane, Washington. They estimated over 150,000 people in less than five years came to Spokane from all over the world and he ministered to them in his healing rooms. He would take people into these rooms and pray for them. He was a very intelligent man, a very scientific, analytical person. He always wanted to know why things happened the way they did. He was not just a naive unintelligent faith healer. He was very sincere in his search for scientific data.

"He went to one of the large laboratories in San Francisco where they had this highly sensitive electronic equipment that would pick up brain waves, or energy waves, and register them on a gauge. They were trying to determine what kind of energy the human body had in it. There was a person in the hospital who had an injured leg. Dr. Lake said that he felt that, if they would give him an opportunity, he would show them that the power of the Holy Spirit, that flowed through him when he layed his hands on people for healing, could be measured. They took their electronic equipment and connected it to this man's leg.

Dr. Lake said, 'I'm going to pray. I'm going to lay my hand on this man's leg. When I do, I want you to watch the needle on your electrical equipment.' When Dr. Lake layed his hand on the man's leg, the needle registered all the way to maximum. It was "scientifically" documented that there was a tangible flow of power that came from Dr. Lake into this man's leg. With all their previous experiments, they had not experienced anything with such dynamic force.

"This shows that there is a wonderful power that

flows into a person's body, and the same thing that the doctors are now proving scientifically, God has been using through His servants for thousands of years."

CHAPTER XVI

"The Man—Vic Coburn What Is He . . . Really?"

My favorite American writer is Sinclair Lewis. I have read his books as well as everything about him I could come across. Probably he, more than any other source, encouraged me to write. He was asked once how one goes about writing a book. Lewis said it was the simple art of applying the seat of one's pants to the seat of a chair; the implication being that writing demands boundless time, energy, and dedication.

I was impressed more with the way Sinclair Lewis went about the task of preparation for writing than I was with his finished products. To write a book such as *Main Street,* he first selected a small town and lived there for a period to get the "feel" of a small town.

Then he drew his own fictitious town down to minute detail. He put his town on the wall so he could see it as he wrote. Next, he selected the characters who would populate his town. He could keep a diary of all his characters, listing every detail of each person: their physical characteristics, their habits, their slightest idiosyncrasies. He did this to make certain he never let a person speak or act "out of character." Before he began page one of *Main Street,* he already had his town and the people in it. He knew the kind of people they were.

Main Street, from inception, was locked into his people in his town. He followed a similar procedure with every book: the preacher with *Elmer Gantry,* the middle aged conformist businessman with *Babbit,* etc.

Although his research was always full and well rounded, Lewis' finished product always turned out to be a black and white photograph. He always ended up with only one side of a town, or a preacher, or a businessman, or a doctor, or a lawyer; and usually it was the bad side. This was because Lewis was a no-good son of a gun. As a person, he was obnoxious, ill-mannered, inconsiderate, insensitive, unfair and, in many ways, almost driven toward visciousness. As a result, he ran through marriages and friends like a bulldozer, and finally, died alone in a hospital outside Rome after spending the last thirty years of his life as an alcoholic.

I make no apology for confessing that I have enjoyed reading Sinclair Lewis or that I have drawn inspiration from the energy and dedication with which he applied the seat of his pants to the seat of a chair.

I do not pretend to be in his class as a writer. I do not expect ever to be awarded the Nobel Prize for literature, as was he. I only hope that I will never be guilty of producing the kind of one-sided photographs of human beings as did he.

In presenting this view of a faith healing ministry in general, and Vic Coburn specifically, I have tried to give a picture in full color, showing all sides. I was not commissioned by Vic Coburn to tell his story in his words. He can do that. Nor, was I commissioned by his opponents to slip up on his blind side and create a subtle expose. Others can attempt that, if they choose.

A subject such as faith healing, which involves a rupturing impact upon the human personality—either for good or for ill—and effects such a vast portion of a nation's population, deserves attention and investigation. Any man who already has established, and will in the future command a dominant position of influence in the religious life of a nation, deserves similar attention and investigation. Whatever conflicts or paradoxes that result from the study are left to the reader to resolve. I came neither to praise Vic Coburn nor to bury him; only to help people know him and what he does.

A SELF–MADE MAN

Vic Coburn has many characteristics that are consistent with other outstanding men of faith in previous years, both within and without the faith healing context. Although he had very little formal education, he is an extremely well-read person. He devours books. He keeps books on numerous subjects around him at all times. He has a searching, inquisitive mind. In a conversation, he will ask a dozen questions.

Vic tries to learn at least ten new words each week. His vocabulary rivals almost anyone you will meet, other than Spiro Agnew. This kind of striving, in words and books, is usually found in a man who, for various reasons, had his formal training cut short. This type person bears out the axiom that what a man learns, or that a man learns, is more important than where he learned it.

In the style of self-made men, Vic is not neutral on any subject. What he knows, he knows for certain, and what he believes, he believes for sure. In preaching, this is a powerful weapon, for it translates itself to people in the form of authority. It was said of Jesus Christ that He spoke as one having authority. We know that Jesus Christ, as a man, didn't know everything.

He didn't know the earth was round; at least He didn't tell those in His day, if He knew it. But what He knew, He knew for certain.

Most of all, He knew what was in the heart of man, and He transmitted this insight with authority.

Maybe this is the point where God picks up on the self-made part of man and uses it for God-made purposes. What keeps people coming back to Vic Coburn's services night after night is that he appears to know what is in the heart of man. To me, this does not require a mind reader. It rather requires a man who has dedicated his life to viewing the needs, questions, shortcomings and desires of the human heart from God's perspective. Vic Coburn has apparently given himself to this task.

A MAN IN TOUCH

Why write a book about Vic Coburn? What's so special about him? I recall someone asking Wilt Chamberlain's manager one time what he (Wilt) was like? He replied, "oh, he's just like any other black, seven foot, millionaire basketball player."

What's so special about Vic Coburn? Nothing more than any other person who is heard personally by thousands of people each night, seen on television by millions of people each week, and receives thousands of letters each day.

Of these three, the mail is the one aspect not under public scrutiny. Vic has a publication, "Deeper Faith," that is presently mailed into several hundred thousand homes each month, both in America and in Canada. The mail ministry has grown to sufficient dimensions to require Vic to curtail some of his crusade activity to give it more personal attention.

In a ministry such as Vic's, the mail takes on a peculiarly significant importance. There are basically two types of ministries. We will call them, for sake of clarification, evangelistic, and deliverance. An evangelistic ministry has, as its primary goal, the gaining of converts. This type ministry basically uses the mail to solicit contributions to help win more people to Christ. A deliverance ministry has the two-fold emphasis of salvation and healing. The minister is seen as one who prays for people's needs—spiritual, emotional—and physical.

Vic's is a deliverance ministry. The mail, therefore, becomes predominantly "problem mail." People write and share things that they would pay a psychiatrist $50 an hour to share with him.

This type mail puts a double burden on a ministry. Certainly many of these people send contributions to the ministry. But they have mainly been assured they will receive help and relief regarding their problems. If the help does not come, the help stops coming from them financially. If a man were only interested in getting contributions, he would not risk this support on whether God was going to help the persons who offered their financial help.

Strangely enough, there is a value that begins in this type mail ministry before a person like Vic Coburn even receives the letter. There is such a thing that some psychiatrists have called "extemporizing one's rottenness." It is a crude-sounding phrase, but descriptive none-the-less. It refers to the fact that often one has taken the biggest step toward the solution of a problem when he has the courage to get it out into the open—to share it with someone else. Very often a person can write down on paper that which he could never bring himself to say to another person. This is an essential initial value of a mail ministry.

A letter can become a powerful point of contact. One woman wrote Vic and described to him the extreme pain she had been having. Later, she wrote another letter which, with her permission, Vic allowed me to read.

"For three days," she began,"I walked the floor in pain, waiting for your response to my letter. I knew that when the postman arrived with your letter, I was going to be healed, because you had prayed for me. One day the postman walked up to the door and handed me your letter. Before I finished reading it, my pain was gone. God had healed me. I am now rejoicing. I have been delivered of my pain. It has not returned."

This type story is multiplied a hundred-fold in the weekly mail ministry of Vic Coburn. Some are very unsophisticated, almost illiterate. Others are apparently highly sophisticated and intelligent. They write because they feel they have nowhere else to go. They send a personal plea for help and get a personal response. In an age that is given to impersonalization—Zip codes, credit cards, social security numbers—this mail point of contact carries a personal benefit that is purging, cleansing, and apparently to many people, highly rewarding.

If a person sends a contribution, that is his perogative. If he sends nothing and uses Vic's postage paid return envelope, the response still comes.

This may be the most inexpensive form of help that is available today. The only way to find out, I suppose, is to write Vic Coburn, 9229 Sunset Blvd., National City Bank Bldg., Los Angeles, California, and see if it benefits you.

A MAN WITH FRIENDS AND ENEMIES

Just as Vic Coburn is not neutral on any issue, people are not neutral about Vic Coburn. He attracts some and repells others. He is a man from God to some and of the devil to others. People either love or hate this type man. They either want to help him or destroy him.

At least Vic is in good company at this point. People were not neutral regarding Jesus Christ while He was on the earth. They were either for Him or against Him. Strangely enough, He attracted the ones you would have thought He would repell—the hard core down and outers; the sinners; and He repelled the ones that one would have thought He would attract—the highly religious.

In His case, Jesus gave the reason for this: He was a help to the sinner and a threat to the religious.

Vic Coburn has many friends, namely those who have been helped through his ministry. Beyond these, the life of a man in a ministry such as Vic's is not only a lonely one by the very nature of being a public figure, but also lonely from the standpoint that there are so many people who, for various reasons, continually attempt to undermine both the man and the ministry. One would be tempted to see this as nothing but a good case of paranoia on the minister's part, but it is more than that.

First, there is the normal core of hucksters and con men who follow ministries such as this. There are men who travel like gypsies from ministry to ministry. They come under the guise of experts in various fields. They write good letters; they compose good magazine copy; they are specialists in advertising, and on and on. What they really are, in most instances, are frustrated failures who couldn't make it big on thier own and turned, as a last resort, to the making of a fast buck in the glow of a man who did make it.

These men come to a person like Vic with two credentials: they love God and feel they have been sent by God to help him. They always follow a similar pattern. They get inside the ministry. They render such tireless energy and attention that they work themselves into a position of trust. They then proceed to find ways to rake off a little for themselves here and there. They pass some business along to fellow hucksters in the printing, photography, advertising, travel, or hotel business. They learn to figure an extra hidden markup for themselves. Vic pays the tag at both ends. Soon they drop subtleties and try to steal: money, equipment, postage, books—anything of value.

The minister finally catches them. They repent and fall on their face asking forgiveness. Foolishly, the minister gives them another chance, not realizing that it was not a mistake they made, but their business they were pursuing.

Finally, the minister says they have to go. At this point, love in the huckster dies; blackmail is born. They begin to infer that they have seen or heard things within the ministry that the public should not know. They would hate it if they were put in a position where they have to depart on an unfriendly basis.

What they usually know that shouldn't be told is nothing. Still, this legion of gypsies go from ministry to ministry spreading untruths, half-truths, and false impressions about their previous employers, all the while looking for a new object of their undying trust and devotion.

I wanted to go into this matter because it represents

one of the greatest injustices which I have found, not necessarily regarding Vic Coburn, but with numerous ministers and ministries. Most of the derogatory information that has been spread about numerous popular ministers has been fostered by this band of hucksters, for malicious and vindictive self-serving purposes. Since my company primarily represents ministries, I have had the unfortunate experience, not only of meeting, but having been taken by some of these persons. If I were not too busy, I would name a few names, seek a few lawsuits, and try to smoke a few out. It would do no good. They are too many. As with cockroaches, one must simply spray regularly and put each one that survives out of the house as quickly as possible.

A second group of enemies, to a minister like Vic, is preachers. These men are not hucksters. Nor are they liars and thieves. They are simply small men who do not understand what it is that grew a Vic Coburn so big, and at the same time stunted their growth. Their principle flaw is that they wanted to be big also. And they have concluded that the easiest way for them to gain stature is to bring the Vic Coburns down to their size.

Vic will be the first to admit that some of his staunchest opponents today are some of his minister friends who first encouraged him into the ministry, This is all very sad, and really not worthy of further discussion. It is simply a part of the fabric that helps wrap a Vic Coburn in a lonely existence.

A third group of enemies to a Vic Coburn ministry is the general circle of religionists who do not happen to believe as Vic does. There is nothing so divisive as differences in religious belief. History records all this. People have been drowned, hanged, and burned at the stake for religious differences. Wars have been fought because of religious differences. Probably more blood has been shed along the Gaza Strip than any other piece of real estate in the world: the land that is called The Holy Land; and all in the name of religion.

It is probably easier to make a target of a faith healer than anyone else. He is usually charged with preying on the hurts and hopes of the helpless. I recall what Oral Roberts once said at a World Congress on Evangelism. I am paraphrasing but this was the substance of his statement:

"Before you criticize me for praying for the sick and dying, remember this: I am usually the last resort for these people. They have already been to the doctors; they have already been to the psychiatrist; they have already been to other ministers. If I turn them away, they have absolutely no place else to go, and nothing left to do but count the hours until the grave swallows them up."

Some of my friends have asked me why I decided to write a book like this. I always reply, "I don't know. I just wanted to do it." Maybe the above is the reason. I'm just a fellow minister who grew weary of all the times he was shot at himself; who decided to grab a rifle and circle the wagons with the Vic Coburns of the world.

Another more prestigious, but none-the-less formidable opponent to a Vic Coburn, is the manager of the local television station. It may surprise you to realize that it is extremely difficult for one like Vic Coburn to secure time on many television stations. The reason involves no set policy, but rather the strangest form of irrational and inconsistent censorship one can imagine. Larry Coyle, Vic's television agent and producer, has to battle for practically every minute of T.V. time he secures for the evangelist. Larry recently passed along an example of the inconsistency that is involved here. I asked Larry what was the main reason that stations gave for rejecting Vic's T.V. program. He told me that most stations resent the laying on of hands. They do not mind what a man says as long as he does not touch another person on camera. Strange.

Then Larry recounted an incident that occurred recently: a station put Vic's program on the air, and then, after a few weeks, took it off. When Larry pressed for the reason, he was finally told that a viewer had called and criticized the program. The program was being shown about midnight on this station. Think of it! One old man, victimized by insomnia, sitting in a darkened room by his T.V. is allowed to be a board of censorship of one, regarding what America will and will not see over television. And so the old man was left to his nightly bloodbath of violence via T.V., free from viewing a man whose only claim is that God has given him a healing touch.

A MAN WITH A DREAM

Most men fail in life before they even get started, not merely because they didn't dream, but because they didn't dream big enough.

For five years, I was the minister of The First Baptist Church in Altus, Oklahoma. While there, I met a man named Cal Buckley, who was the editor of the *Altus Times Democrat*. One night Cal told me this story. When he was thirteen years old, he had a paper route. He said, "every afternoon I would return from throwing my papers and sit on the steps of the *Times Demo-*

crat with some of the other paper boys. I would sit there and say, 'some day I am going to be the editor of the *Altus Times Democrat.*'

Cal went on to say, "C. A., I am now forty-two years old, and the editor of the *Altus Times Democrat.* And I have only one regret: that back there, when I was thirteen, I was not saying, 'some day I am going to be editor of the *New York Times.*'"

Vic Coburn is a man with a dream; a big dream. He wants to be the editor of the *New York Times.* He wants to do the biggest work for God of any man in history, not because it will bring him fame, but because no man's work, thus far, has been enough to bring the world to Christ.

Television is an integral part of his dream for it is the most far reaching and powerful means of communication known to man at this stage in history. It is a costly dream, as we have already discussed. It is a time consuming dream involving hours of preparation and production each day. A dream involving television places almost super human demands on one's creativity. One can preach the same sermon week after week in crusades, but not on television. The major networks spend millions of dollars each month just to find fresh material and new stories. Vic Coburn is his own sponsor, his own story writer, his own source of creative supply.

Vic Coburn's dream, as he has related to me, is to see the world saved and well in his day. "I will not be content," Vic says, "merely to say that I want to do my very best. My best will never get the job done. Rather, I want to be an instrument through which the great commission can be fulfilled in my day. I have asked God to allow me to present the saving, healing, strengthening power of Christ to the entire world before my ministry is finished. And I believe He is going to allow this to happen. The stage is set. The door has been opened. If I will keep myself fit and usable as God's servant, I know He will do His part."

A MAN WITH A HEALING TOUCH

The phrase, "a healing touch," did not originate with me. All my life I have heard it said of certain physicians, "he has a healing touch." If God is the Great Physician, it should not be out of place to say of a minister that he has a "healing touch."

Vic Coburn does have a healing touch. When I use this phrase, I am not merely speaking of his laying on of hands. It is that and more.

It has been said throughout history that certain persons have, what is called an "ontic quality." This term refers to the peculiar, innate power within certain individuals to move persuasively over others. The quality has not been confined solely to ministers. Certain actors have been said to have it. Certain lawyers have had it. Very few men in any profession have had such a quality, certainly very few ministers have had it, but those who did, made an indelible mark on the age in which they lived.

It was said of Reverend George Truett, an esteemed minister of several decades past, "When he talked, men listened; when he finished, they moved."

When Vic Coburn talks, men listen; when he finishes, they move. And in ways I do not fully comprehend, and known only, I suppose, to God, Vic, and those to whom it happens, when Vic touches lives with his message, his prayers, his hand, they are never the same again.

Beyond this point, there is little else for me to say. I am not a prophet. I have no way of knowing where the years will take this young man. The final chapter is in his hands, and those who are touched by his ministry. Regardless of what happens, I will never be sorry that I wrote this book.

As I write these final pages, I am in India. I am surrounded by people who are not only starving, but are diseased through and through. It is not only startling, but bewildering to me that the world's riches are so unevenly distributed—riches not only in dollars, but in food, truth, and health.

When a man comes along who feels he has been called of God to tackle the entire job—with or without the help of others—who am I to place one straw in his path?

Perhaps I have been guilty, in the movement of this story, of giving Vic too little space to present his message. Therefore, in order that the reader might get a better grasp of the man first hand, I am going to attach some of Vic's messages to the appendix. I will leave you here in the hope that some light has been shed on a subject that has perplexed man through the ages: God and man, and their relationship to one another.

APPENDIX

Sermons by Vic Coburn

I

"The Healing Compassion of Christ"

The greatest thing Jesus did while on this earth, was to reveal the "Divine Compassion" of God His Father to a sick and sinful humanity. The Law of Moses was demanding and exacting, as all laws are. But Jesus Christ came into the world as a revelation of the LOVE AND COMPASSION of God!

God's great soul was moved with divine love as he looked upon a needy world gripped in the clutches of Satan and sin. The Bible tells us that the COMPASSION of God was so great for the LOSTNESS of humanity "That He gave His only begotten son, that whosoever believeth in Him, should not perish, but have everlasting life" (John 3:16).

Some people are inclined to think that God is careless about the world, but this is not so. He cared so much, that He offered the most priceless TREASURE in Heaven to redeem mankind from the slavery of sin. According to the scriptures, God valued our souls to be worth "More than the WHOLE WORLD AND THE FULLNESS THEREOF!"

When the great multitude followed Jesus into the wilderness, He was moved with COMPASSION, for they were like sheep having no shepherd. The disciples wanted to send them away because there was not enough food to feed such a large number of people. But Jesus cared for these people, He understood humanity. He was moved with compassion because the people were hungry and in need. God is deeply concerned about every area of our lives! He has made divine provisions for us in His Word. Jesus promised that the Father knows we have need of the material things of life. As we seek FIRST the kingdom of God and His

164

righteousness, ALL the necessities of life will be provided for . . .

Jesus taught the world to have compassion. It's easy to love the lovable, and the beautiful person, but Christ told us to have COMPASSION! This kind of compassion radiates the Healing Power of God.

One day they brought to Jesus a woman who had been caught in the act of adultery. They said, "According to the law of Moses, she should be stoned." According to the law there was no HOPE FOR HER! But the COMPASSION of Jesus reached out to that sinful woman. He said, "Go and sin no more."

THE HEALING POWER OF COMPASSION

A poor dying leper came running to Jesus one day, falling before his feet he cried out, "Oh Lord, if thou wilt, thou canst make me clean!" Jesus looked down upon this man with penetrating eyes of love and was moved with COMPASSION. He reached out His healing hand and touched him, saying, "I WILL; be thou clean." THANK GOD, for the healing will of Christ! This story tells us why Jesus saves and heals. He is MOVED WITH COMPASSION! DIVINE COMPASSION.

"Jesus Saves and Heals!
He is moved with Compassion,
DIVINE COMPASSION"

Compassion reaches further than the law, further than mere sympathy. COMPASSION reaches to the very heart of LIFE ITSELF! Divine Compassion was the secret to Jesus' ministry. His compassion was what drew the multitudes to Him. They saw in Jesus more than just another religious leader, they saw that He really CARED. His love and compassion was ever bringing healing and deliverance to the captive soul and body.

When I read of the healing ministry of Jesus, it is too hard for me to understand how religious teachers today can stand by the bedsides of the dying and afflicted and tell them that they must be patient and suffer pain and agony for the glory of the Lord. Jesus HATED SICKNESS! He destroyed it everywhere He went. He healed EVERY disease and EVERY sickness. To the preacher who has the audacity to tell people they must suffer for the glory of God, I ask one simple question: "Does it seem logical that Jesus who went about healing ALL who were sick and oppressed of the devil, now uses the thing He HATED to bless those that He gave His very life for?" Can sickness be anything but the will of HATE and EVIL?

The compassion of Christ brought LIFE and HEALING. That wonderful life and healing is available to you! If you have never experienced the power of His healing presence, you can this very day. Regardless of your physical need, Christ will meet that need. Maybe you have sinned and need forgiveness, ask Jesus to forgive you. "If we confess our sins, He is faithful and just to forgive us our sins". . . (1 John 1:19).

PRAYER OF COMPASSION

The greatest need in the heart of God's ministers is compassion. The church has become too much of a dead institution, filled with rules and regulations, instead of the living body of Christ flowing with DIVINE COMPASSION. How often have Christians prayed for the needs of others without sensing even a spark of compassion? The Bible tells us that "Faith worketh by LOVE."

A few years ago, God revealed to me the difference between merely praying for someone to be healed or delivered and praying for them WITH THE FLOWING COMPASSION OF CHRIST. One night during a prayer line, a little child came before me for prayer. Its precious little body was tormented with a devastating disease. I started to lay my hand on the child and pray, but suddenly, I heard Jesus say to me, "What if this was one of your children, how would you pray then?" My heart seemed to literally MELT within me. I looked at that little tormented child through different eyes! All I could think of was what if that was my little daughter? The COMPASSION of Christ swept through my soul. I layed my hand on the child and the power of the Holy Spirit flashed from my right hand into that suffering body and instantly a miraculous healing occurred. From that night, I have understood the power of the "PRAYER OF COMPASSION."

Before I pray for the sick, I must feel the flow of Christ's compassion in my heart. "Faith worketh by LOVE." The gift of healing within my life is never stronger than when this compassion is moving in my very soul. When I lay my hand on someone, I actually feel this compassion surging from me into the the person I am ministering to. I can't explain this to everyone, but I know it is the secret to God's healing power.

THE COMPASSION OF THE CROSS

Jesus said, "Greater love hath no man, than he that is willing to lay down his life for his friends." Christ's consuming compassion drove him to suffer death for our sins. His example on the cross, is forever set before us as the proof of God's Divine COMPASSION! After they had pierced His hands and pierced His feet, with His last breath He prayed to God: "Father, forgive them, for they know not what they do."

Jesus was able to look upon the faces of His murderers, and plead for their forgiveness. This kind of compassion goes beyond the compassion of mere man. The human heart is not capable of giving forth such love. This type of compassion is MIRACULOUS! It comes only from the divine nature of God Himself.

Dear friend, your life may be distressed by the torments of sickness or the conviction of sin. Even as you read this message, your heart and mind cries for the compassionate touch of Jesus. I feel the Holy Spirit flowing through my soul as I write this . . . I know God desires to minister to you right now! Open your heart to Christ, let His compassion and power flood your body, mind and soul! Whatever your need is, turn it over to Christ in faith. TRUST IN HIS DIVINE LOVE FOR YOU.

Philippians 4:19 declares, "But my God shall supply all your need according to His riches in glory by Christ Jesus." This glorious promise is for you! The riches of Heaven are at your disposal, if you will only turn those needs over to God and trust in His unfailing care for you.

TURN-LOOSE of your problems and give Jesus a chance to help you. God has already provided an answer to your need, but he is waiting for you to accept it. God is not BANKRUPT, He is still God ALMIGHTY!

God's concern for you was proven on the cross. I believe you feel the HEALING COMPASSION of Christ as you finish reading this message. I pray God, by His wonderful Spirit, will give you a MIRACLE RIGHT NOW!

II

"Understanding the Nature of Faith"

"Faith is the substance of things hoped for and the evidence of things not yet seen" (Hebrews 11:1).

Many people are confused about the true significance and definition of faith. Some believe the word faith merely means the kind of religion you subscribe to. Others can give long theological and theoretical definitions of what they think faith is all about. But what is faith? In addition to the Bible's definition of faith in Hebrews 11:1, faith is TAKING GOD'S WORD AT FACE VALUE, believing that He is not a liar. If He has spoken, HE WILL bring it to pass!

True faith, the kind that bases its belief upon the foundation of the faithfulness of God, is the greatest power in the entire universe. God has placed His omnipotence in the hands of DARING FAITH! Whenever a man or woman is found who dares to exercise the power of "Living Faith", the mighty works of God are manifested in a marvelous way.

Every Christian should be living a life of victory and spiritual strength, but instead, many are living powerless and defeated lives because they have not understood the nature of faith. Without a concept of faith, it is impossible to have the ability to believe in your heart.

Thousands of Christians pray religiously every day, but their prayers seem to go unanswered. They become frustrated and discouraged in their prayer lives; the joy and excitement of prayer has left them. These people are living lives void of expectancy. If an answer to one of their prayers does come, they are shocked and amazed! Christianity to them has become nothing more than mere routine, something to do on Sundays.

No true born-again, spirit-filled Christian need ever live this type of life! Christ died to make us "MORE THAN CONQUERORS!" Anyone, including a small child, can easily understand and use the power of "Living Faith." Many confuse themselves by thinking that hope and faith are the same. We all need hope, but let us not confuse hope with what the Bible clearly teaches about faith.

Hope is passive and uncertain, but faith is very POSITIVE and aggressive! Hope says it may happen, FAITH SHOUTS, "IT WILL HAPPEN!"

The key to victory is not the passive talk of hope, but the powerful and positive CONFESSION OF FAITH. Hope waits for God's blessings to become real some day; FAITH takes them NOW! Many people are bound by sickness and disease who have little or no faith that God will heal them NOW. They hope for recovery; they may even confess that someday God in His own time will make them whole. On the other hand, faith does not set idly by hoping for deliverance; instead, faith boldly confesses "By His stripes I AM HEALED" (Isaiah 53:5).

No, my friend, faith and hope are not the same. The nature of faith accepts the promises of God at face value. Real faith does not rely upon natural reasoning, it relies entirely upon "THUS SAITH THE LORD!"

Although hope is an important part of Christianity, it can never adequately substitute for the power of "LIVING FAITH". Nothing but bold daring faith can drive the believer through the raging storms of life to experience the great joy of spiritual victory. With the strength and confidence of true scriptural faith abiding in your heart, you can command the most furious storms of life. "PEACE BE STILL!" Jesus spoke these powerful words into the face of a raging storm nineteen hundred years ago while He and His disciples were out on the sea in a small ship. The maddening wind and waves obeyed His voice and the Bible says, "THERE WAS A GREAT CALM!" Your storm WILL OBEY YOU! Take courage in the strength of Christ, you can use the power of "Living Faith" to defeat and calm the winds and waves of adversities that come against you.

I WON'T BELIEVE IT UNTIL I SEE IT

How often people are defeated by these words. Many have the misconception that it is wrong or even dishonest to claim something prayed for if the evidence cannot be seen with the natural eyes. But here is where thousands of Christians have not understood the true NATURE OF

FAITH. "Faith," according to Hebrews 11:1, "is the substance of things hoped for and the EVIDENCE of things NOT YET SEEN!" You may not be able to see the evidence immediately with your natural eyes, but through the peerless power of faith, you HAVE THE EVIDENCE in spite of the testimony of your senses!

Nothing pleases God more than for us to accept His Word as true, even before His promises are made good, or become physically evident to us.

Jesus said, "What things soever ye desire, when ye pray BELIEVE that ye receive them, and ye shall have them." (Mark 11:24) He did not say, ". . . when ye pray HOPE that ye receive." Hope and faith are not synonymous!

Only the power of LIVING FAITH will move the mighty hand of God. The Heavenly Father longs to save, heal, and bless, but He asks only that you believe His unfailing promises.

Many have complicated and misunderstood the simplicity of LIVING FAITH. As I mentioned in the previous chapter, real faith is merely TAKING GOD AT HIS WORD, believing that He is not a liar! Jesus declared, "Heaven and earth will pass away, but my Word will NEVER PASS AWAY! God's Word is eternal, therefore, we can rest assured that His promises will not fail us!

I am constantly amazed at Christians who will accept the word of their doctor, dentist, lawyer, and banker, but who will doubt the faithfulness of God for no good reason. We usually trust a person as far as we can trust his reputation and integrity. Has God ever given us a reason to doubt His honesty and integrity? NO! A THOUSAND TIMES NO!

III

"The Power of Healing Faith"

The reason thousands of Christians are sick and suffering from the torments of disease, is because they have never been taught the positive message of divine healing. If Christians were taught as unwaveringly about healing as they are about God's willingness to save the vilest sinner, the high rate of sickness and disease in the church would be abolished!

Jesus Christ "took our sins in His own body that we being dead to sin, might live unto righteousness, and by whose stripes we were healed" (1 Peter 2:24).

The Father has planned that every believer should be a conqueror over sickness and the works of the devil, but only a few have accepted their Calvary-purchased inheritance.

Many ministers of the gospel teach and preach that although God does heal some, we can't always be sure it is His will to heal everyone. They sit by the bedside of the sick and dying assuring the suffering victim that God must surely be working something out for His glory. These same preachers will boast of believing and teaching the WHOLE BIBLE. They declare that Jesus Christ, "Is the same yesterday and today and forever," but in the same breath, DENY the modern day miracles of a risen Christ."

Faith for divine healing cannot be exercised while a person is bound by traditional doubts regarding God's will in physical healing. Perfect faith can only be built by KNOWING that God has promised something and that He desires to fulfill that promise.

Jesus Christ was God's revelation of healing and compassion in the flesh. The Bible says, "The Son of man was manifest in the flesh that He might destroy the works of the devil!" Also, we read in Acts 10:38 "God anointed Jesus Christ of Nazareth with the Holy Ghost and with power: who went about doing good and healing all that were oppressed of the devil."

When Christ was on this earth, He revealed the Father's will concerning physical healing and deliverance. Jesus' ministry was a "HEALING MINISTRY!" He spent more time healing the sick and casting out demons than He did anything else. He did not heal the sick just to prove His power as some teach, but He healed then as He heals today, because HE WAS MOVED WITH COMPASSION!

I have preached this simple message of complete deliverance to countless thousands nation-wide, and without one exception, wherever people have given heed to the Word of Faith, the results have been astounding! We have witnessed over fifty deaf people receive perfect hearing in one service. As many as ten blind people have received their sight in a matter of minutes. I have prayed for over a thousand people in a single service resulting in hundreds of outstanding healings and miracles.

The "HEALING POWER OF CHRIST" is as available today as it was when He walked the face of this earth! God's Will has not changed during the past nineteen centuries. He is still the great "I AM—I AM THE LORD THAT HEALETH THEE!" (Exodus 15:26)

THE CONFESSION OF FAITH

Without CONFESSION, a person's faith is powerless! Confession is what brings POSSESSION, because you confess with your mouth what your heart BELIEVES. "Out of the abundance of the heart, the mouth speaketh" (Matthew 12:34).

In Romans 10:10 we read, "For with the heart, man believeth unto righteousness, and with the mouth confession is made unto salvation."

NOTICE: Paul says, "CONFESSION is made unto salvation," Salvation does not become a conscious fact until AFTER CONFESSION is made.

Many people struggle for faith because they have not understood the powerful principal of CONFESSION. Confession is simply agreeing with God: saying what His Word says. Confession is faith's way of expressing itself!"

Many people are only willing to confess what they can see or feel; they refuse to confess what they believe would be a lie. But when you confess your salvation or your healing before you see or feel the actual evidence, this is not lying, for you are only saying what GOD HAS ALREADY SAID IN HIS WORD! Faith does not need a special feeling or a physical evidence, because we read in Hebrews 11:1, that, "Faith is the substance of things hoped for, the EVIDENCE OF THINGS NOT YET SEEN!"

Salvation could never become a wonderful reality in a person's heart if that person refused to confess his faith in Christ with his mouth. Rev. 12:11 tells us that those who overcame the devil did so, "Through the blood of the lamb and the WORD OF THEIR TESTIMONY." This means they overcame Satan's powers as Christ did in the wilderness, by using the WORD OF GOD as their CONFESSION.

TALKING DOUBT ALWAYS BREEDS MORE DOUBT

People get in a habit of talking defeat and weakness; their confession becomes one of failure. And the more a person talks weakness, the weaker he becomes. The more he talks failure and defeat, he becomes a greater defeated-failure.

I personally believe that we glorify the DEVIL when we constantly testify to our sicknesses and weaknesses. Instead of declaring the ability of God, we are confessing the power of Satan—giving him more praise than God our Heavenly Father. May I further add that you can become BOUND by

174

what you confess. You will never be delivered as long as you talk bondage and captivity!

I'm sure you know someone who is constantly complaining about everything. This person lives a life of negativism and pessimism—always looking for and expecting the WORST! These kinds of people live lives of anxiety and fear because they have become bound by a CONFESSION OF DOUBT. Confession can work two ways, it can either be a powerful tool of spiritual victory and deliverance, or it can destroy a person's faith and defeat his spiritual life.

WE UNCONSCIOUSLY TALK ABOUT
WHAT WE BELIEVE

Faith always talks about the thing prayed for as though the answer had already come—even if the evidence cannot be seen with the natural eyes.

When I pray for a person's healing, I can usually determine their faith by what they CONFESS. If they are uncertain regarding God's will for their healing, they will confess with their mouth that unbelief. Of course, there are exceptions to every rule. I have heard some people boldly confess their positive faith that they were going to be healed, but they were not healed. Why? Because their confession was a FRONT! If your confession is not backed by faith within your heart, it is powerless.

God and His Word knows no defeat, neither must you! If you feel defeated over some circumstances in your life, don't confess it, instead confess Romans 8:37, "We are more than CONQUERORS through Christ." If you are bound by a sense of weakness, don't confess that weakness— rather CONFESS "I can DO ALL THINGS through Christ which strengtheneth me" (Phil. 4:13). You can have the powerful ability of God unleashed within your very life! You CAN'T know defeat or weakness by confessing the WORD OF GOD.

Begin to TALK FAITH TALK, give up your old confessions of doubt and unbelief. Those burning temptations can be overcome by confessing "Greater is he that is within you, than he that is within the world!" That sick and suffering body will be healed by the power of God—if you will stop waiting for healing—and by faith and a POSITIVE CONFESSION take your healing by confessing—"BY HIS STRIPES I AM HEALED!"

IV

"Prayer Power"

"THEREFORE I SAY UNTO YOU, WHAT THINGS SOEVER YE DESIRE WHEN YE PRAY, BELIEVE THAT YE RECEIVE THEM, AND YE SHALL HAVE THEM" (MARK 11:24).

Scientists believe that nuclear energy is the most powerful force in the universe, but they are wrong. PRAYER is the greatest power in the universe! God has placed His omnipotence in the hands of every praying Christian.

Armies have been defeated and kingdoms have been pulled down through the power of prayer. Satan's kingdom suffers its greatest defeats as a result of a praying church. The devil stands stripped of his devastating authority before the weakest Child of God who knows how to use the mighty weapon of prayer. The church of Jesus Christ has made its most world shaking advances when its members have empowered the message of the cross by intercessory prayer.

The most effective strategy of Satan throughout the history of the church has been to convince Christians that "PRAYER IS NOT IMPORTANT." He has succeeded in stripping many preachers of their spiritual power as a result of this deceptive strategy. The servant of God can only be an influence for Christ as long as his life is saturated with the anointing of the Holy Spirit, and this anointing can only be obtained through a close relationship to God through prayer.

Prayer is the only weapon that Satan FEARS and RE-SPECTS in the hands of the Christian! As long as the devil can keep the church from intercessory prayer, he can continue to hold millions in the slavery of sin and sickness. Only a church that is empowered with the reality of the Spirit of God can bring deliverance to an oppressed world. PRAYER MOVES THE HAND OF GOD.

One writer said that "God did nothing in the world, but in response to prayer!" A close study of the scriptures in both the Old and New Testament will reveal that God demonstrated His power usually when His people or one of His servants prayed. FAITH and PRAYER move the mighty Hand of God! Miracles should be commonplace in the church, but because of a lack of prayer and simple scriptural faith, many who profess to be Bible believing Christians have never witnessed an authentic miracle of God.

God longs to manifest himself in the form of answered prayer. He wants to show Himself "STRONG IN OUR BEHALF" but His hands are tied by the prayerlessness of the church. Even Christians who have been raised to believe in the power of prayer, have today fallen into the rut of formality and religious ritual. There is a desperate need for a PRAYER REVIVAL throughout America and the world. A prayerless church is a DEFEATED CHURCH."

Early in my ministry I discovered that a strong prayer

life was the secret of a strong ministry. The Holy Spirit taught me to spend much time before the Lord in prayer and fasting. As the years have passed, prayer has become as much a part of my daily life as eating and sleeping. It is the source of a fruitful and Christ exalting ministry. Many Bible schools and seminaries need to spend more time teaching the powerful principles of prayer, than they do teaching theological hair-splitting.

Whenever I have had the opportunity to talk to any young minister about the work of the preacher, I have always emphasized two very important things: daily consistent prayer, and fervent prayer. I have seen many entire cities become aware of the power of God as a result of BINDING—SPIRITUAL—PRAYER.

During the past two years, I have learned that it is impossible to reach a city or area for Christ until first the spirits of opposition are bound by prayer and fasting. I never begin a crusade with confidence until first I have literally gone into the "SPIRIT WORLD" and taken authority over demon opposition through intercessory prayer.

Recently, God spoke to me on the way to a crusade. I was deeply concerned about the stiff opposition we were receiving from various political sources in the city. I was trying to figure out how to defeat this opposition when all of a sudden, God spoke these words to my spirit, "For though we walk in the flesh, we do not war after the flesh: For the weapons of our warfare are NOT CARNAL, but MIGHTY THROUGH GOD to the pulling down of STRONG HOLDS!" (This is a scripture found in 2 Corinthians 10:3-4.)

After this message came to me like an exploiting REVELATION, I looked up 2 Corinthians 10:5 and read further where it said, "Casting down imaginations and EVERY HIGH THING that exalteth itself against the knowledge of God." I had always believed in the power of intercessory prayer, but now a new understanding of my God—

given authority in prayer began to burn in my heart. I suddenly realized as never before what the key to world RE-VIVAL and EVANGELISM was. Only PRAYER POWER will move this generation toward Christ!

HOW TO RECEIVE ANSWERS TO YOUR PRAYERS

Effective and powerful prayer involves more than saying a lot of faithless words to God. Some church members pray to be heard of men rather than God. Only the prayer that is sincere and intensively directed to God in faith will be rewarded with an answer. God is no different than you or I in one respect; when you are talking to Him and He is communing with you, He wants your undivided attention. I have never liked someone to look off and get interested in something else when I was talking to them, I am sure you feel the same way. The Bible says the "Effectual Fervent prayer of a righteous man availeth much." This scripture implies that HALF-HEARTED praying will get you nowhere.

No sincere prayer of faith will go UNANSWERED! Jesus challenged us in Matthew 7:7 to expect a positive response to our prayers, "Ask, and it shall be given unto you; seek, and ye shall find; knock, and it shall be opened unto you; for everyone that asketh receiveth; and he that seeketh findeth; and to him that knocketh, it shall be opened."

God is not a respector of persons! He requires the same of every person; FAITH. He desires to bless us and meet our needs, but the Bible says, "We have not because we ask not!" According to Jesus, our part in prayer is to ASK; God's part is to GIVE. The Heavenly Father delights to give His children "EVERY GOOD and EVERY PERFECT GIFT." Jesus said, "The thief cometh not but to KILL, to STEAL and DESTROY, but I am come that you might have it more ABUNDANTLY" (John 10:10). Prayer opens the reservoir of GOD'S ABUNDANT LIFE!

ACCORDING TO GOD'S WILL

"And this is the confidence that we have in Him, that, if we ask anything according to HIS WILL, He Heareth Us; and if we know that He Heareth Us, whatsoever we ask, we know that we have the petitions that we desired of Him" (1 John 5:14). Praying according to the perfect will of God is the KEY to answered prayer! But how do you pray according to God's will? Some believe that you must have a special revelation or spiritual witness to know God's will. Wo do have a SPECIAL REVELATION: THE BIBLE! God's perfect will for your life is contained in the scripture. We don't need a greater revelation than "thus saith THE WORD OF GOD!"

When we ask God to forgive us our sins, we have confidence that He will, because of His unfailing and eternal promises to us in His Word. "If we confess our sins, God is faithful and just to forgive us of all sin, and to cleanse us from all unrighteousness" (1 John 1:9). When we ask God for physical healing, we can rest assured of that healing because of His many promises in the Bible. "The prayer of faith shall save the SICK, and the Lord shall raise them up" (James 5:15). . . . "Himself took our infirmities, and bare our sickness" (Matt. 8:17).

A simple definition of real prayer could be this, "Asking God to do what He has already PROMISED to do in His word!" When we have a financial crisis in our lives we can stand upon the promise of Philippians 4:19, "But my God shall supply ALL your needs according to His riches in glory by Christ Jesus."

When I pray, many times I remind God of a certain promise in His Word. This gives me an unwavering confidence that my prayer will be answered. You see, praying according to God's revealed will, automatically guarantees an answer to your prayer!

NOT YOUR GOODNESS BUT HIS GOODNESS

The Bible teaches us that if "our hearts CONDEMN us

NOT, then have we CONFIDENCE towards God." A false sense of unrighteousness or self-condemnation will destroy the power of prayer in a person's life. One of Satan's most effective and destructive tools is CONDEMNATION. If he can succeed in condemning us by false accusations, he knows our faith will be shattered, thus making our prayers powerless against his kingdom.

When we come before God in prayer, it is not because of our righteousness or meritorious deeds that He hears us, but it is because of our redemptive righteousness through Jesus Christ! This is the reason that only prayer offered in the name of JESUS will receive the attention of the Father.

When Christ was preparing to leave this earth, he left us the promise of PRAYER POWER through His wonderful Name. "And whatsoever ye shall ask in MY NAME, that will I do, that the Father may be glorified in the Son." "If ye shall ask ANYTHING in my name, I WILL DO IT!" (John 14:13-14).

When we pray in Jesus' name, we are enwrapped in His righteousness! There is no need for CONDEMNATION, for "There is therefore now no condemnation to them which are in Christ Jesus, who walk not after the flesh, but after the Spirit" (Romans 8:1).

My dear friend, take YOUR PLACE as God's child today! The divine nature of Jesus Christ dwells within you. Take NEW COURAGE. Begin to use the mighty PRAYER POWER that God has given you! CHALLENGE that mountain to MOVE through the irresistable AUTHORITY of the NAME OF JESUS CHRIST!

V

"The Prayer of Faith"

In James 5:17, we read, "The PRAYER OF FAITH shall save the sick and the Lord shall raise them up." This scripture shows us the wonderful power of prayer when backed by FAITH.

Many people have confused the issue of prayer, they have been led to believe that prayer must be a vigorous exercise of one's vocabulary. A consistent petitioning of God for the thing desired . . .

Because of such misconceptions thousands of Christians have never enjoyed the thrill and excitement of praying the PRAYER OF FAITH and witnessing the power of God work in their behalf.

God never intended for just a few people to have FAITH, but rather that every member in the Body of Christ should be a CONQUEROR through the power of Living Faith! In my crusades across the country, I am constantly teaching and encouraging my audiences to use THEIR OWN FAITH for deliverance. I feel this was what Jesus attempted to do; build personal faith in the hearts of those He ministered to. WHAT IS THE PRAYER OF FAITH?

The prayer of faith is merely asking God to do something that He has already promised to do in His word, then believing that He is FAITHFUL WHO PROMISED! In Matthew 7:7, we are challenged to "ASK AND RECEIVE." Our part is to ask, God's part is to GIVE! That sounds simple doesn't it?" Well, that is how simple prayer really is. Prayer is actually CHILD'S WORK. Jesus said, "except ye humble yourselves as little children . . ."

Concerning the prayer of faith many people have the

idea that this always means an immediate answer. They think unless INSTANT results occur, the prayer of faith has not been offered. I am sure many have failed to receive healing for their bodies and answers to their prayers because they have tried to dictate just how and when they wanted to be blessed. I have seen thousands of prayers answered instantly, but I have also prayed and no immediate results were forthcoming. But my faith does not stand on what I see or hear, but rather what God HAS SAID IN HIS UNFAILING WORD! For this reason, I know that every PRAYER OF FAITH will positively receive an ANSWER, whether instantly or by gradual process it makes no difference, THE ANSWER MUST COME!

The secret to the prayer of faith is after you have asked God in Jesus' name to do a certain thing—then be BOLD TO CONFESS God's Word, ". . . Nothing shall be impossible to you" (Matt 17:20) : and, "If ye abide in Me, and My Words abide in you, ye shall ask what ye will . . . and it shall be done unto you" (John 15:7). Also, Jesus promised, "If ye ask anything in My Name, I will do it" (John 14:14). According to these scriptures, you have a legal right to confess that your prayer has been answered even before you see or hear the physical results.

FAITH VERSUS REASON

The natural mind is faith's most lethal enemy. Your mind has been taught to only accept what can be backed up by the five senses. But our senses have NOTHING TO DO with real faith. FAITH ignores our senses! The Bible tells us that we walk the Christian life by FAITH and not by SIGHT. We must consider God's Word as true even when our natural senses disagree.

Many times after prayer has been offered to a sick person, the symptoms may linger for awhile. The person who is ruled by his natural senses will believe the evidence of the symptoms over the promise of God's Word, but faith will smile unwaveringly and declare "IT IS DONE."

When you have fully complied with God's Word, and offered the prayer of faith, you may rest assured that God has heard you and that the victory is ALREADY YOURS even before you see it, feel it, or hear it" FAITH is not afraid to take a STAND on the promises of God even when the natural mind whispers, "IMPOSSIBLE, you dare not claim something that you cannot see." Most Christians are bound by sense knowledge, they say that they are living by faith, but when sickness strikes the first thing they do is call the doctor or take some medicine. When financial problems arise, instead of looking to God to supply their needs, they immediately apply for a bank loan.

The PRAYER OF FAITH is taking God at His Word! Begin TODAY to cast your natural doubts and reasonings aside, stop looking for HOT FLASHES and COLD CHILLS to convince you that God has answered your prayers. Faith is not feeling nor is feeling faith! The only witness you need that your prayer will be answered is the FAITHFULNESS OF GOD! You can hang YOUR SOUL ON THE WORD OF GOD!

FAITH IN REVERSE

Some people don't realize it, but they are using their faith in REVERSE. That's right, in REVERSE! These people will refuse to accept anything from God until they can see the evidence with their natural eyes.

But in complete contrast, they are living a reversed faith life. Let me explain. For instance, a mother whose little Billy has just come home from playing with little Johnny down the street who has been sick with the chicken pox, will immediately begin preparing for her child to come down with a case of chicken pox. This mother does not have any special witness that her little boy will become sick, but she uses her faith in reverse and accepts it SIGHT UNSEEN!

Thousands of Christians have accepted the devil's diseases by faith! Many of God's children live tormented lives of affliction because they have never learned how to use their faith in the RIGHT DIRECTION. You see, faith will work for you two ways. There is negative faith and POSITIVE FAITH. Negative faith always believes and EXPECTS the worst and usually ALWAYS GETS IT! POSITIVE FAITH, leans confidently upon the unfailing promises of God's Word, even when natural reasoning and circumstances SHOUT IT SHALL NOT HAPPEN!

I have seen people whose entire lives were bound by negativism and wrong believing. Usually these precious people never enjoy the wonderful power of true Christianity and spiritual reality. These people seem always defeated and discouraged, unable to overcome the daily problems of life.

The person who uses the POWER OF LIVING FAITH in his life will have battles and trials like everyone else, but Christ's VICTORY will always be HIS VICTORY! Spiritual CONQUEST will be a daily REALITY in his life!

YOU CAN HAVE GOD'S FAITH

Although faith "cometh by hearing, and hearing by the Word of God," it is still a supernatural GIFT OF GOD. The Bible tells us that "God hath dealt to EVERY man the measure of faith." We could not receive Jesus Christ as our Lord and Saviour without the FAITH OF GOD. It is His ability to believe that enables us to do exploits through the mighty name of Jesus.

God wants you to have HIS FAITH within your heart! According to the scriptures, the most pleasing thing to God is a LIFE OF FAITH. Doubt dishonors God and His Word, but faith glorifies and exalts the integrity of His promises.

In Mark 11:22, Jesus said to His disciples, "Have faith in God." The true translation of this verse is actually,

"HAVE THE FAITH OF GOD." Stop and think about this a moment! Jesus is offering each of His disciples the power of His FATHER'S FAITH. The same faith that enabled Christ to work the works of His Father while on earth. He offered to those who followed Him! God's FAITH knows no impossibility! With His faith in YOU, ALL THINGS are possible.

In Mark 11:23, Jesus describes the irresistible power of the Gift of Faith.

"For verily I say unto you, that WHOSOEVER shall say unto this mountain, be thou removed, and be thou cast into the sea; and shall not doubt in his heart, but shall believe that those things which he saith shall come to pass; he shall HAVE WHATSOEVER HE SAYETH!" I believe the term mountain was used by Jesus in this verse to power-fully illustrate the fact that if FAITH can move a real mountain, then there is NOTHING unmoveable in our lives! Certainly sickness, Satanic oppressions, financial despair, persecution, and many other things seem mountainous at times, but Jesus promises that the POWER of God's FAITH in our hearts will enable us to literally SPEAK TO OUR MOUNTAINS to be REMOVED, and they must obey us!

My friend, BEGIN using God's faith TODAY! Christ died to make YOU more than a conqueror! Pull yourself together, shake off the dust of despair and defeat. Get your eyes off past failures and impossibilities. LOOK to God and His unfailing promises for NEW STRENGTH. Jesus Christ DEFEATED defeat on the cross! He is the AUTHOR and FINISHER of your faith. Allow the Holy Spirit to build in your heart by the promises of God, FAITH FOR DELIVERANCE. I want to challenge you to start a NEW LIFE; a life of LIVING FAITH! I thank God for allowing me to discover early in my ministry the powerful principles of faith. Miracles have become a daily way of life for me. If you will apply the simple teachings of faith that I have written in this book to your own life, PRAYER and Christian LIVING will become exciting realities. Remember, THINK FAITH, TALK FAITH, ACT FAITH!

"Therefore, I say unto you, WHAT THINGS SOEVER ye desire, when ye pray, BELIEVE that ye receive them, and ye SHALL HAVE THEM" (Mark 11:24).

VI

"Victory Through Praise"

One of the greatest sources of Spiritual power and victory available to the Christian is PRAISE. Nothing will unleash the reality of Christ in your soul like communicating the THANKSGIVING of your heart to God in sincere worship.

The phrase "Praise the Lord" is used so lightly by some in the church, that the true meaning and significance of its power and purpose has been lost. During the years I have traveled as an evangelist, I have had a growing conviction that one of the greatest needs in the church is a RESTORATION OF JOY! Wherever a church is found that emphasizes PRAISE and SPIRITUAL WORSHIP, there is always a REVIVAL SPIRIT and souls are being won to Christ.

Many Christians have lost the wonderful FLOW and

FREEDOM of the Holy Spirit in their lives because of a fear of being over emotional. But this need not happen; true PRAISE is not making a spectacle of one's self. Praise is the most beautiful experience a child of God can have in his relationship with Christ through the Holy Spirit. Only the Christian who develops a PRAISE LIFE can enjoy the full joy of his salvation. Satan has succeeded in giving some Christians a spiritual complex regarding public or even private worship. He has convinced them that only religious fanatics orally and outwardly express their praise to God.

Nothing will spark a flame of revival in the individual's heart or within a congregation of believers like the practice of true THANKSGIVING and PRAISE! In Psalms 22:3, we read, "But thou art holy, O thou that INHABITETH the praises of Israel." Here we see that God actually possesses the praises of His PEOPLE! When a person turns his mind and emotions towards God in praise, the spirit of man makes contact with the Spirit of God, thus punctuating the presence of the Holy Spirit in the person's life.

I have seen many people who were bound by a spirit of defeat and discouragement, wondrously delivered after discovering the POWER OF PRAISE. You see, often a person who is discouraged will pray for release and victory, but seemingly nothing happens. As a result of this constant defeat, some people become frustrated and even angry with God. Their faith gets weaker and weaker, doubts and fears begin to possess their minds and spirits. But Christians NEED NOT BE DEFEATED! Here is the Bible's solution for spiritual discouragement; "REJOICE EVERMORE!" "IN EVERYTHING GIVE THANKS."

In order for us to sincerely praise the Lord, we MUST BE THANKFUL and we can only be thankful as we learn to accept *LIFE AS IT COMES!* I'm not suggesting that we should let the devil run over us while we merely lay passively in the middle of the road, but I am saying that there is great victory for the person who will COMMIT every aspect of his life to God in THANKSGIVING.

In my personal life I have discovered the victorious power of a daily PRAISE RELATIONSHIP with God. Early in my ministry, I was frequently defeated in prayer, because I couldn't always feel the liberty and freedom that I thought was necessary to pray effectively. Many times I would feel so cold and powerless when I attempted to pray and as a result, the devil would talk me out of my victory and confidence. But one morning when I went to pray, and I experienced this spiritual bondage, instead of giving up in defeat, I lifted my hands and heart to God in praise and thanksgiving! At first, there was no difference in the way I felt, but I continued to MAGNIFY the Lord for all that He had done in my life. Suddenly it seemed as though the mighty FLOODGATES of Heaven were opened and the glory of the Lord was poured upon my soul!

After this experience, prayer became a NEW JOY! I had discovered a secret that enabled me to pray with greater power and faith. From that day until now, I have always begun my sessions of prayer with PRAISE AND THANKS-GIVING. Christians could enjoy the power of prayer so much fuller if they would learn that there is more to pray-ing than merely asking God to do THINGS FOR THEM. Our relationship with Christ, like a successful marriage, must be a GIVE AND TAKE proposition. He delights to give us "ALL THINGS THAT PERTAIN TO LIFE." But in return, He longs for us to express our love to Him in PRAISE!

UNLIMITED POWER OF PRAISE

"Blessed is he who submits to the will of God; he can never be UNHAPPY. Men may deal with Him as they will . . . He is without care; He knows that 'all things work together for good to them that love God, to them who are called according to His purpose.' "—Martin Luther.

God his intended that Christianity should be a "NEW LIFE" of victory and conquest. Only the devil rejoices when we live defeated and powerless lives; he is continuously accusing us of sins and shortcomings in an attempt to make us feel and confess unrighteousness. Millions of Christians live under an oppression of CONDEMNATION! They are constantly struggling to be more holy in order to please God, thus merit His blessings. Did you know there is only one righteousness that God recognizes: HIS RIGHTEOUSNESS IMPARTED TO US THROUGH JESUS CHRIST!"

When we receive Christ as our Lord and Saviour, He becomes OUR HOLINESS and because of His shed blood, we are blameless in the eyes of God. "According as He hath chosen us in Him before the foundation of the world that we should be HOLY and WITHOUT BLAME before Him in love" (Ephesians 1:4).

Other people may only see you as you are, you may only see yourself as you are, but God looks at us differently! He has made us a NEW CREATION for His own glory and praise—we have been made perfect in God's eyes through Jesus Christ.

Doesn't the realization of our righteousness in Christ BRING PRAISE TO YOUR HEART? I am not talking about the pride of self-righteousness, but the wonderful reality of God's righteousness in us!

We are free to PRAISE AND WORSHIP God without the sense of sin or condemnation. Don't be ashamed to come before the Lord with a feeling of SONSHIP and UNLIMITED POWER.

True praise builds faith in your heart, enabling you to release the power of the Holy Spirit in your life. You reach a place when you are no longer struggling in prayer begging God for answers, instead, you are praising God for His miracles even before you can see them!

As Martin Luther said, you are blessed and happy when

you submit the cares of life to the WILL OF GOD. Nothing can shake you! "You are more than a CONQUEROR THROUGH CHRIST" (Romans 8:37). There IS UNLIMITED SPIRITUAL POWER available to the Christian who will "IN EVERYTHING GIVE THANKS!" You can begin praising defeat and discouragement right out of your life!

DELIVERANCE THROUGH PRAISE

The Bible is filled with stories and examples of the POWER of PRAISE. God has revealed His delight and willingness to bring DELIVERANCE to anyone who will believe His word and accept His unfailing promises. Nothing EXPLODES the power of faith in a person's heart like the wonderful spiritual joy and release of true praise!

In the sixteenth chapter of Acts, we read about Paul and Silas being placed in the Philippian jail after being beaten and falsely accused. The atmosphere of the dark and dirty cell they were in, was everything but bright and encouraging. They had every reason to be discouraged and despondent about their circumstances. But instead, I can see these two men of faith and optimism bgein to talk about the power of Christ which brought deliverance to them so many times in the past.

It's easy sometimes to look around us and allow our problems and circumstances to become unmoveable mountains of defeat. But the authentic power of Christianity is only truly proven when we "PUT THE PROMISES OF GOD TO THE TEST!"

Paul and Silas were in the dark confines of prison, but they knew that "Whom the Son of God has set FREE, he is FREE INDEED!" Only their bodies were in captivity, their souls and spirits were still free to praise the Lord. In the glorious liberty and power of the Holy Spirit, the Bible says, "And at midnight Paul and Silas prayed and sang PRAISES unto God; and the prisoners heard them!

And suddenly there was a great earthquake, so that the foundations of the prison was shaken and immediately ALL THE DOORS WERE OPENED AND EVERYONE'S HANDS WERE LOOSED."

These two men of God had learned to accept LIFE AS IT CAME! They knew they were in God's will in spite of being in jail, therefore they could lift their hearts in praise right in the midst of apparent defeat. Regardless of the perplexing circumstances in YOUR LIFE, turn your emotions and mind to God in worship and thanksgiving "For we know that ALL THINGS WORK TOGETHER FOR GOOD to them that LOVE GOD, to them that are called according to His purpose" (Romans 8:28).

VII

"God Wants to Heal You"

Until you are fully convinced that God wants you to be a WELL person, there will always be plaguing doubts in your mind regarding your own personal deliverance. And, until you can have faith for healing it will never come. But don't despair, because faith in God's healing power is so easy to have and exercise! As you read this chapter, you will begin sensing a new and personal faith filling your very being.

Let me first ask you a simple, yet important question, "IS GOD HONEST OR NOT?" What I mean is this. Do you think God will do what He says He will do? I am almost certain your answer is positively YES!

All right, then all we have to do is establish in our minds what God thinks about your sickness. Does He will that you be sick or does He want you to be healthy? Some would have us believe that sickness is a blessing sent from God to work out His will of love in our lives. But what does the Bible teach regarding sickness and your deliverance?

In III John 2, we read, "Beloved, I wish above all things that thou mayest prosper and be IN HEALTH . . ." You see, we are God's cherished children. He loves us with a divine love that drove Him to send Jesus Christ to die on a cruel cross for our sins. Would you place sickness upon your child for any reason? Would you torment your little boy or girl with some diabolical disease just because they did something wrong? You know you wouldn't! Then how could you even think that God could do such an un-God-like thing? The Bible teaches us, "That evil men, being evil will give good gifts to their children, HOW MUCH MORE will your Heavenly Father give good things to His Children!"

No sane earthly parent would afflict a child with cancer or some other destructive disease. So, why should we believe that the greatest FATHER of all would desire any of His obedient children to be sick.

A WONDERFUL GOD OF HEALING AND HEALTH

Even a casual study of both the Old and New Testaments of the Bible reveal that God has always been "THE LORD THAT HEALETH THEE" (Exodus 15:26). In every generation God has manifested His marvelous healing power wherever He found men and women who would have faith in His word.

Regarding the scripture, Exodus 15:26, mentioned above, they were the words God spoke to about three million people, the Israelites. Everyone of these people believed the words that God spoke. The results are found in Psalms 105:37, "He brought them forth . . . and there was not

ONE FEEBLE PERSON AMONG THEIR TRIBES."

Can you imagine three million people all well and strong? Not one weak or sick person!

Dear friend, if that could happen under the law, is it too hard to believe that it can happen now? We are living under grace, mercy and truth. Jesus died to make us free from both sin and sickness. "Himself took our infirmities and bare our sicknesses" (Matthew 8:17).

"Himself took our sins in His own body upon the tree, that we being dead to sin, might live unto righteousness, by whose stripes YE WERE HEALED!" (I Peter 2:24).

Sickness and disease are taking their terrible toll upon the bodies of countless thousands of God's people. This should not be, but the average teacher and preacher is doing nothing about it. They stand by the bedsides of the sick and dying with nothing but words of sympathy instead of words of healing authority. These faithless preachers and teachers make excuses for their powerless prayers, by assuring the suffering victims that God is surely working out something in their lives for His glory because of their sickness.

This is the trend of present-day ministers, that I wish to disprove and boldly challenge. Instead of merely sympathizing with the sick, I use the compassion and faith of Christ to bring God's healing power to them. My message is simply this, "IF YOU ARE SICK, GOD WILL HEAL YOU . . . AND IF YOU ARE SINFUL, CHRIST WILL WONDROUSLY FORGIVE YOU!"

THERE IS HEALING FOR EVERYONE

Some precious people believe wrongly that God wills to heal some, and not others. But nowhere in the entire New Testament of the stories of Jesus' own healing ministry do we ever read where He refused to offer His healing power to anyone who came to Him in faith. In only one story do we read where a poor man desiring healing for his

194

leprous body cried out, "Lord if thou wilt, thou canst make me clean" (Mark 1:40).

In this story we read where Jesus was moved with compassion and stretched forth His hand and touched him saying "I WILL; BE THOU CLEAN!" God is no respector of persons. If He will save one, He will save ALL! If He will heal one, He will heal ALL!

In James 5:14-15 we read, "Is ANY SICK among you? Let them call for the elders of the church; and let them pray over them, anointing them with oil in the name of the Lord: and the prayer of faith SHALL SAVE THE SICK AND THE LORD SHALL RAISE THEM UP . . ."

When Jesus gave His followers power to heal the sick, He did not tell them to heal some, but rather He said "Into whatsoever city ye go into . . . HEAL THE SICK THERE-IN!" The disciples' healing ministry was offered to everyone that would believe their message of Christ and the Kingdom of God. Healing is still for everyone who will accept the person and promises of Jesus Christ!

The greatest faith destroying words I have ever heard are "Lord, if it be thy will." Real faith can never be demonstrated in your heart until you are fully convinced of God's will. The Bible says, "This is the confidence we have in God, that if we ask anything according to His will, we know that He HEARETH US!"

The only way you will ever know what God's will is regarding your life, is by reading or hearing His word. The Bible plainly reveals God's perfect will for your life! Jesus Christ was a revelation of God's will in human form. When Jesus healed the sick and set the captives free, it was revealing to you and me that God wanted to heal us! He wanted to set us free from sin and Satan.

The message of the New Testament is one of COM-PLETE DELIVERANCE, both body, mind, and soul! Healing is for all and should be preached to all. In Luke 4:40, we read "When the sun was setting, ALL they that had ANY sick with diverse diseases brought them unto Him: and He laid His hands on EVERY ONE OF THEM and healed them." Not one person was left out! You don't have to be left out either!

In all the years of my own ministry, I have seldom ever seen a person fail to receive healing either instantly or gradually when once they saw and understood God's will regarding physical healing. This is the most important step to receiving your own healing. You must first believe that God wants to heal you, then you must be willing to act on that faith and boldly claim your deliverance in the wonderful name of Jesus. I promise you that God is faithful to His unfailing Word!

The Bible says that, "God is more willing to give, than you are to receive!" Actually God wants to heal you more than you desire healing! He paid a great price to purchase healing and salvation for you—therefore, He is MORE THAN WILLING to bestow these great and priceless gifts to you this very MOMENT.

HEALING IS IN THE ATONEMENT!

The death of Jesus Christ on the cross was to offer mankind a two-fold work of God's grace. Healing for the soul and healing for the body.

Physical sickness and death came about because of man's fall from grace in the Garden of Eden. Adam and Eve subjected humanity to both spiritual and physical death as a result of their high treason against God. Sin and sickness was not known until Adam fell from God's grace.

The Bible says, "That because of Adam, we all die, but because of Jesus Christ, we shall all live!" Adam's fall brought about spiritual and physical death, but the substitutionary death of Christ has brought deliverance for both sin and sickness!

We read of God's healing atonement in Isaiah 53:4-5; Matthew 8:17-18, and I Peter 2:24. The Hebrew word which is rendered "griefs" in Isaiah 53 is said to be everywhere else in the Bible translated "sickness."

The word "bare" in Matthew 8:17 implies substitution-suffering for our sins and sicknesses. If Christ "bare" our sickness and disease why should we bear them?

In Deuteronomy 28, we read that sickness was given as a part of the "curse." But in Galatians 3:13, we see that "Christ hath redeemed us from the curse of the law." This means that the very cause of sickness has been destroyed by the redeeming power of Christ! We are LEGALLY FREE from the torments of sickness! It's not God's will that you suffer the humiliation and pain of disease and affliction. "Whom the Son of God sets free, HE IS FREE INDEED!"

With such a glorious knowledge of God's perfect will regarding your physical health, you need not pray, "God heal me, IF it be thy will." If, implies doubt, and doubt cancels the power of faith. YOU KNOW it is God's will to heal you! All you must do now is RECEIVE YOUR HEALING IN SIMPLE FAITH! ASK AND BELIEVE!

VIII

"The Supplying Power of God"

Are you concerned about the energy crisis? Millions of Americans are! The whole world is running short of its vital energy supplies. The governments of the nations seem to have no workable solutions. The Bible offers us a wonderful solution to the present shortages of life. The Spirit filled child of God does not need to worry about the energy and food crisis, because God has no "POWER SHORT-AGE"!

Jesus taught that Chrisitanity is a wonderful life of abundance and TOTAL SUPPLY. He declared that He had come to ". . . GIVE LIFE AND GIVE IT MORE ABUNDANTLY!" (John 10:10) You and I who serve God are not second-class citizens. We are the sons and daughters of the LIVING GOD! We are His ROYALTY through Jesus Christ!

Peter said, "GOD HATH GIVEN US ALL THINGS THAT PERTAIN TO LIFE." This means we have a constant supply line from God to us that continually flows His blessings and abundance into our lives. We are not bound by the same economic principles that the world is bound by, for our SOURCE is not of this world, but of AN-OTHER WORLD! The Bible says in Philippian 4:19. ". . . my God shall supply ALL YOUR NEEDS according to His riches in glory by Christ Jesus!"

For many years, Christians have lived under a false bondage, because they have been taught that POVERTY and PIETY were tied together with a very short rope. But this is untrue! God wants His children to prosper in this life. Listen to what the Bible says in 3 John 2, "Beloved, I wish above ALL THINGS, that thou mayest PROS-PER . . ."

The Heavenly Father created the earth and the fullness thereof for an inheritance of the righteous. We are His chosen people. He chose us through Jesus Christ to be His heirs on this earth. Therefore, we have a legal God given right to EXPECT our physical and material needs to be supplied from the abundance of heaven's bountiful store-house. In the sixth chapter of Matthew, Jesus talks about how God feeds the fowls of the air and clothes the grass and lilies of the field. He said, "ARE YE NOT MUCH BETTER THAN THEY?" (v. 26) "Wherefore," Jesus went on to say in v. 30, "if God so clothe the grass of the field, which today is, and tomorrow is cast into the oven, shall he not much more clothe you, O ye of little faith?"

"BUT SEEK YE FIRST THE KINDOM OF GOD, and His righteousness; and all these things shall be added unto you" (Matt. 6:33).

This one scripture spoken by Jesus is the KEY to living the ABUNDANT LIFE OF GOD. When we give our best to God, He then gives us HIS BEST! His best is much greater than our best. The Heavenly Father longs to bless and prosper you, but He has established certain laws that must be obeyed.

These laws are without respect of persons. They are eternal and UNFAILING. There is the law of grace and salvation which promises forgiveness of sin for every repentent soul. There is also the law of divine healing which God has established for every sick and suffering person. This law provides physical health for every person who will in simple faith accept and believe the promises of God's Word.

There is ALSO A LAW OF PROSPERITY that the Bible CLEARLY teaches! This is one of the most misunderstood and neglected laws in the entire Word of God. Few Christians have ever completely understood the potential power of this law. You see, God knew that the material needs of life would be one of the most important concerns of humanity; therefore, He has PROVIDED for His children ALL THINGS THAT PERTAIN TO LIFE!

"The earth is the Lord's and the FULLNESS THEREOF." And God did not place all the vast wealth in the earth for the devil and his crowd. Even as God gave Adam and Eve access to all the resources of this world's abundance, He has given us a never failing supply source for all our physical needs. "BUT MY GOD SHALL SUPPLY ALL YOUR NEEDS ACCORDING TO HIS RICHES IN GLORY BY CHRIST JESUS."

In order for you to understand clearly how the law of

God's SUPPLYING POWER WORKS, I am going to out-
line the simple steps you must follow:

First: You must look to God as the supplier of your
every need. This is the most important step.
You can never reach the front door of God's
abundant storehouse unless you are willing to
look completely to Him in faith to supply your
needs. But remember God is your supplier,
not your job, business or any other source.

Second: You must be willing to GIVE TO GOD
FIRST! For the Bible clearly sets forth the
principle of sowing and reaping. "Whatsoever
a man sows, that shall he also reap." Jesus
"Give and it shall be given unto you, good
measure, pressed down, shaken together, and
running over." Paul said in II Cor. 9:6, "He
which soweth sparingly shall reap also sparingly; and he which soweth bountifully shall reap
also bountifully."

Third: You must direct your giving towards SOUL
WINNING. Mere charitable giving is not
what God blesses. He only blesses our giving
to its fullness when we provide Gospel seed
to be sown by our financial giving. We are
stewards of God's money; therefore, we are
responsible to see that our giving is directed to
the place where it will do the most good for
the Kingdom of God's sake.

These three simple, yet very important, steps that I have
outlined for you will enable you to GUARANTEE God's
supplying power in your daily life. It is an exciting adven-
ture to live a life of faith, depending upon God to supply
your every need, both spiritual and physical.

A FARMER WHO TOOK GOD AS HIS PARTNER!

A few months ago, when I was in Phoenix, Arizona, I heard about a Christian farmer who had just received a fantastic miracle from God. The citrus crop around the Phoenix area had been destroyed because of frost. But one man's cop grew and flourished in spite of the frost. It was this Christian farmer who had taken God as his partner.

The Phoenix newspaper ran a story about this man, and the other area citrus farmers were astounded because their crops were destroyed and his were not. When asked why his crop was spared the destruction of the frost, the Christian farmer replied, "I have always put God first in my living and giving. Therefore, He miraculously saved my crop from the frost."

What happened to this one farmer has happened to many other people who have dared to put God first in their living and in their giving. In the book of Proverbs we find a wonderful promise of God, "Honour the Lord with thy substance and the first fruits of all thine increase; so shall thy barns be filled with plenty, and thy presses shall burst forth with new wine" (Proverbs 3:9-10).

MANY WITNESSES TO GOD'S SUPPLYING POWER

Every day I receive thrilling letters from people who have experienced the marvelous supplying power of God. These precious people write to tell me how God has answered their prayer needs with a miracle. Some have need of physical healing, others need salvation for loved ones, while others need jobs or better jobs.

Sometime ago, a wonderful young couple who had pledged a considerable large sum of money to my ministry told me of a miracle that had happened to them as a result of putting God first in their giving. They had written a post-dated check when they had made their pledge to God for our T.V. ministry. The check was dated for about a month later, and they didn't have the money to cover the check until the very day that it was dated. God miraculously supplied this need.

But then something else wonderful happened. They needed $7,000 to go into a new business, and from an unexpected source, God abundantly supplied this need. They believe this was the abundant overflow that God promised he would pour out upon those who would "GIVE THEIR FIRST FRUITS" to Him in faith.

In a recent crusade, a sponsoring pastor and his wife gave a one–hundred dollar check to help meet the many crusade expenses. I knew when they gave that they really couldn't afford to give that much, but I knew God would bless them for it. Therefore, I prayed for them that God might miraculously return it back to them, even in greater measure.

Well, He did just that!! The very next morning, this pastor and his wife found $150 stuck between their front door! This was $50 more than they had given just the night before.

I could write an entire book on experiences of God's SUPPLYING POWER that I have seen happen in my own life and ministry.

GOD'S SUPPLY MADE NATION WIDE-TELEVISION POSSIBLE!

When I heard the voice of God tell me to plan the "Day of Miracles" television ministry, I knew it would take many miracles to make such an outreach a possibility. I also knew God was NOT BANKRUPT! I knew He would provide the money and material that was necessary.

We stepped out on faith to obey this tremendous call of God to reach millions through nation-wide television. One night, my wife and I sat alone discussing the great cost for starting such a ministry. I turned to her and said, "Honey, if we have to sell everything we own and borrow money to sign necessary papers (television contracts) to go on the air, we will." She gripped my hand and just looked at me, but I knew she felt the same way. Both of us have always been willing to give everything for the cause of the gospel.

When we were married, I had an old 1953 Chevy that had four bad tires. We traveled across the country in this old car conducting revivals. Some weeks we hardly made enough to meet our expenses, but we were happy.

Although God has blessed us today with nicer things, we both feel that same total commitment to the cause of our wonderful Lord. My wife and I are blessed with good health and three beautiful little daughters who love the Lord, and we owe everything to the grace and supplying power of our God.

To make our television ministry a possibility, everyone on my team and staff gave their very best to God. Many of my friends and partners generously gave of themselves and their money to help me go on television. Many thousands of dollars were miraculously supplied in a very short period of time. No one who knows the full story behind this ministry can call it anything but MIRACULOUS.

It is now taking a miracle of God's supplying power each month to keep this ministry going, but God's supply ALWAYS equals our needs!!!

Dear friend, I challenge you to start allowing God to wondrously work within your life in a greater way. He deeply desires to "SUPPLY ALL YOUR NEEDS according to His riches in glory by CHRIST JESUS!"

God knows about all your needs, both spiritual and physical, but He is waiting for you to use the KEYS of blessing and prosperity that He has shown you in His unfailing Word. Open your heart in faith . . . apply these principles that I have taught you in this message, and see what will happen!

REMEMBER THESE THREE THINGS . . .

FIRST . . . Look to God as the supplier of your every need.

SECOND . . . Be willing to give to God first.

THIRD . . . Make sure that you give to win souls.

The Bible says, "God will honour His Word, even above His name." Therefore, you can rest assured that what this message has taught you will be backed up by the SUPPLY-ING POWER OF GOD!